The
Puritan
Mind

BY HERBERT WALLACE SCHNEIDER

Ann Arbor Paperbacks

THE UNIVERSITY OF MICHIGAN PRESS

TO MY FATHER

CONTENTS

THE PURITAN MIND

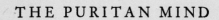

PROLOGUE

The perspectives of history are ever shifting, for human experience, being itself continually subject to change, affords no fixed point of reference for the mind. Not only does each generation find itself compelled to interpret a more or less alien past by the categories of the present, but even this specious present is itself unintelligible unless it be illuminated by the past. Neither the mental world nor the physical has a center and a circumference. The motion of bodies must be measured from points themselves in motion, and the meanings of events are themselves events in a constantly shifting scene. History is, therefore, a world of dark objects pretending to shine by their own reflected light. Past and present are in themselves alike mysterious, but they mysteriously illuminate each other; and though things are never intelligible in themselves, they nevertheless make each other intelligible. This ancient paradox of the human understanding has been celebrated by philosophers from time immemorial. Had they accepted the paradox as a fact, instead of celebrating it as a mystery, the world might contain more wisdom and less philosophy. It may be, as Emerson claims, that "the invariable mark of wisdom is to see the miraculous in the common," but it cer-

3

tainly is the invariable mark of a foolish philosopher to see nothing else.

We shall do well, therefore, to accept without more ado the general fact that the final history of anything cannot be written, and that whatever outline history may have at present will sooner or later be lost in favor of new outlines, for it is the ever-changing present and not the past that gives form to history.

The physical life of man has a certain continuity which the life of the imagination usually lacks. Nature is comparatively stable and the basic human enterprises of getting food, shelter and comfort have a certain similarity in all ages in spite of industrial and political revolutions. But the human imagination wanders off every now and then into paths whence there is no returning. Physical adventures, even when unsuccessful, can usually be repeated, but these imaginative adventures radiate out into the heavens and are for the most part irrecoverable. A world of thought is slowly created, but it may perish overnight. This fate has recently overtaken the mental world of New England. For several generations in this country, fathers and sons understood each other and moved in the same universe of discourse. Samuel Mather in the eighteenth century did not share all the opinions of his great-grandfather, Richard, in the seventeenth, but he worked on the same intellectual material and employed the same ideas. Timothy Dwight in the nineteenth century did not share all the opinions of Samuel Mather in the eighteenth, but he worked on the same intellectual material and employed the same ideas. Nathaniel Hawthorne did not like the ideas of Jonathan Edwards, but he could not afford to ignore them. Today all this is changed: that Puritan New England tradition, together with its problems and ideas, has all but disappeared, and we turn to it, if indeed we do, not because it forces itself upon us, but because we occasionally visit the monuments and tombs of a buried antiquity. Even Emerson, who helped dig the grave, already stands cold and classic, an immortal monument over a buried past. New teachers, new ideas, and other languages, have shaped our minds. Our grand-parents are aliens in our country and we in theirs.

Such rifts in the course of the imagination make a history of the mental life of a people almost as impossible as unprofitable. Indeed the only way to approach it, and the only motive for approaching it, is the selfsame spirit of imaginative adventure. Only an adventure into the flights of the human imagination can discover for us the similar adventures of others. Science and society may evolve continuously, as if carried in some eternal mind and fed by impersonal forces, but philosophy, religion and the other fine arts wander whithersoever the spirit listeth. For the arts are not surplus products of life; they are rather life's very essence. The life of an animal body is a continual venture, and a living imagination is one of its greatest hazards. A mind dies when at rest. Hence even the rational soul must vegetate, and the spirit must be a wanderer. But not all vegetation is reason. The wandering mind may make discoveries or it may merely lose itself. It is, therefore, not enough that we merely attempt to follow the flights of religion and philosophy here presented; such a pursuit is enlightening only in so far as we are enabled to understand why these flights appeared to afford wider perspectives and fresh points of vantage for the lives out of which they arose. But these lives were not ours, and nothing is less enlightening than to attempt to estimate the ideas of other men and ages as though they were made for us. A philosophy is part of a man's person; in it he lives and dies; it is not, save by sheer accident, a disembodied contribution to the evolution of knowledge. Therefore, we shall here be concerned not with truth but with facts; with a series of biographies—the lives and deaths of famous ideas.

No living things can feed on themselves, nor do ideas grow out of the mind. Ideas have a natural soil and a physical habitat. Therefore, to understand both the origin and the fruit of an idea, one must examine the teeming world by which it was generated and into which it falls. One can, of course, follow an idea into its undying dialectical implications without examining the social landscape in which it lived, just as a botanist might study the glass flowers in the Harvard museum. Such an alignment of ideas, according to their appointed niches in the mind's eternal architecture, must not be mistaken for an understanding of their temporal and earthly meanings to those human beings who from time to time held them and in whose lives they played a living part. The skeleton of an idea may be examined by the logician after its death, and his anatomical dissection may incidentally throw light on the mechanics of its life, but such dissection is at best an instrument to the study of its living functions. As an incident in the study of life, anatomy is useful, but as a substitute for it, it is philosophic fanaticism. Neither is understanding produced by gaping and gazing at life's immediate flavors. A living idea is understood when seen in terms of its environment. It is true, ideas are members of that eternal world of lifeless forms; but this is the world in which ideas are entombed and enshrined. The world in which they live is the physical world, in which alone life is possible. If I succeed in sketching the basic themes of Puritanism in America against a background of their social habitat, and in describing the effect of events on the lives and deaths of these themes, I shall leave it to others to dissect the theological bones of a once living religion.

CHAPTER I

THE HOLY COMMONWEALTH

"Christ Jesus intending to manifest his Kingly Office toward his Churches more fully than ever yet the Sons of men saw, . . . stirres up his servants as the Heralds of a King to make this Proclamation for Voluntiers as followeth.

"Oh yes! oh yes! oh yes! All you the people of Christ that are here Oppressed, Imprisoned and scurrilously derided, gather yourselves together, your Wifes and little ones, and answer to your severall Names as you shall be shipped for his service, in the Westerne World, and more especially for planting the united Collonies of new England; Where you are to attend the service of the King of Kings, upon the divulging of this Proclamation by his Herralds at Armes. . . .

". . . Could Casar so suddenly fetch over fresh forces from Europe to Asia, Pompy to foyle? How much more shall Christ who createth all power, call over this 900 league Ocean at his pleasure, such instruments as he thinks meete to make use of in this place. . . . Know this is the place where the Lord will create a new Heaven, and a new Earth in new Churches, and a new Common-wealth together."[1]

[1] Captain Edward Johnson: *A History of New England, or Wonderworking Providence of Sions Saviour* (London, 1654). In Albert Bush-

8

The events which were taking place in Europe and which led to the founding of the American colonies were of too great a magnitude not to arouse the philosophic imaginations of those who participated in them, provided they had any imagination at all. There were those, of course, who broke loose from all their civilized ties, embarked on a perilous ocean, disembarked in a howling wilderness, established themselves there, experienced a thousand dangers, joys, discoveries, and disappointments without giving the whole process a thought. Many were too excited to think, but more were too busy or too blindly driven. There were some, however, whose imaginations were kindled and for whom all these events fitted neatly into an outline of history. Among these men the clergy were preeminent, for in those days it was the clergy who were the professional outliners of history, and the revealers of what in our day is called the grand strategy of evolution, but what in theirs was called the economy of human redemption. History always has been one of the primary playgrounds of the philosophic imagination, and the interest in it has always been primarily pragmatic. Even today, when there is a small class of scientific historians who approach history as other natural scientists approach their subject-matters, and who have succeeded in illuminating historic events by discovering their natural causes, the general interest in their discoveries is still philosophic. We still seek lessons in

nell Hart: *American History Told by Contemporaries* (New York, 1897), Vol. I, pp. 366-7.

history and pretend to be able to discern its outline and the various stages of its evolution. Accordingly the art of prophecy is still a profitable and respectable profession. Today it is the school-teacher, the novelist, the editor of home libraries, the playwright, and the popular writer on science, evolution and sundry other things in which he is not versed, who are shaping our conception of the general scheme of human life. But at the time of the founding of New England, the clergy had almost a complete monopoly of this field. Instead of reading about it in the Sunday papers, as we do today, the old Puritans had a quaint custom of making history six days a week and, on the seventh, "going to meeting" to hear the minister explain it.

Apart from these institutional differences between the Puritans and us, the great gulf which separates their minds from ours lies not so much in their habits of thinking as in the body of so-called facts or data out of which thinking proceeds. For us, human history begins with the anthropoid apes and is organized about the idea of the gradual development of modern civilization out of the life of primitive man, a process which we sometimes call progress, sometimes merely evolution, and which we believe will continue until human life disappears from this cooling planet. No doubt there is more myth and imagination in this picture of history than we are conscious of; future generations may soon be entertained by it, regarding it as another of those pretty myths and epics on which the human mind feeds. On the whole, however, it is constructed out of the facts and records of experience in so far as these have been discovered to us. But the so-called facts and records which were available in the seventeenth century were radically different, and the resultant picture of history was also radically different. Its main outlines were derived from Jewish folk-lore and Hellenic mysticism, the former of which was mistaken for history and the latter for science. According to it, history began in the mind of God, and its structure was essentially moral and dramatic, being the familiar story of the revolt of subjects against their sovereign. The final act, or, as the Puritans called it, the last period, was already far spent. Soon history would give place to final judgment and moral perfection; the villains would be eternally damned, and the heroes eternally united to God, their author and end. Thus to all eternity this epic of God's glory would be recited and admired by God and by all rational creatures who could appreciate dramatic beauty and moral justice.

The general course of this process had been described by Saint Augustine in his *City of God,* but much work still remained to be done on details. Saint Augustine had identified the City of God with the whole body of saints, visible and invisible, under Christ, their heavenly king; this body of saints was easily identified with the church of Christ, and this church, in so far as it was embodied on earth, soon came to be identified with the holy catholic church, and the holy catholic church with the Roman Catholic Church. As long as the Roman Church and the Roman Empire were working together, and as long as their chief task was one of subjecting and civilizing barbarians, this interpretation of history was quite adequate and plausible. Church and empire were not unnaturally regarded as struggling for the redemption of man against the sundry heathen whom the Prince of Darkness kept benighted. But as the struggle changed into a rivalry between the church and the kings of the newly forming nations, the church was forced to fight, not heathen hordes, but powerful princes who called themselves Christian. At this crisis the Apocalypse of St. John came to the rescue with its prophecy of the Anti-Christ. At last the Anti-Christ had appeared! To the subjects of the pope, the king was Anti-Christ, and naturally to the subjects of the king, the pope was Anti-Christ. However, though the Protestant princes were quite willing to accept the theory that the Anti-Christ resided at Rome, and though they did not hesitate to claim a direct, divine right to rule, which from the fall of the Empire the pope had regarded as his exclusive privilege to bestow on those princes who recognized the supremacy of the spiritual kingdom, nevertheless they lacked the temerity to proclaim their own kingdoms to be the City of God. It is true Hobbes' *Leviathan* almost deified the state, but Hobbes' prime concern was to put the state on a purely secular basis. Hobbes was, in effect, undermining the whole scheme of the City of God, and though he protested against being styled an atheist, he was naturally feared as such, since neither Protestants nor Catholics were ready to accept a theory of the state which was merely temporal or secular, and which left out of account the fundamental plot of human redemption. Few objected to his absolutism but all to his secularism. Richard Baxter, for example, wrote: "That Hobbs his Leviathan, or way of absolute Impious Monarchy, . . . tendeth not to secure us of a Righteous Government, is a point that needeth no proof with any reasonable man; were it but because the irreligious Author pretendeth not to any such thing as the securing a succession of the Christian Religion, without which a Righteous Government is not to be expected."[2]

In all this both Papist and Protestant agreed, and precisely because they agreed in theory and differed merely in practical application, they were reduced to such *ad hominem* arguments as "Anti-Christ," "whore of Babylon," and similar mutual vituperation. Theoretically the same is true of the conflict between the Anglicans and the Puritans. Both believed that the state should be maintained in the interest of the City of God, or the church, but in practice they could not agree on what constituted the true church. However on the part of the Anglicans this was the merest theory. An Englishman always has a saving sense of humor and a practical ability to compromise. He knew and privately admitted that the English monarchy was not the City of God and never would be. He knew that both the British state and the Anglican Church were in fact secular in origin and aim. He accepted the estab-

---

[2] Richard Baxter: *A Holy Commonwealth* (London, 1659), p. 225.

lished church so long as it was merely an establishment of the state. He gladly celebrated the religious mysteries, for as such they did not interfere with his secular strivings. In short he was a pious man of the world. Both the Lords Spiritual and the Lords Temporal, though professedly citizens of two distinct cities, were really just English lords and acted accordingly. This balance of worldly wisdom and spiritual hypocrisy, which is largely responsible for the charm of English society and the prosperity of the English nation, was temporarily upset by the Puritans, though they themselves soon recovered it when they became comfortably established in New England. In Old England these aggressive middle-class favorites of God, being both socially and intellectually *nouveaux riches,* lost their traditional balance and sense of humor, and ventured to hope that England might soon become the City of God.

Richard Baxter, one of the boldest of them all, at last took this final step in Protestant philosophy of history and argued that even the British Commonwealth should be turned into a Holy Commonwealth, and in general that the civil state should be identical with the church, the visible City of God. His treatise, *A Holy Commonwealth* (1659), is a consistent, clear exposition of the whole theory. He writes:

"Thes. 24. The world is a Kingdom whereof God is the King, . . . an absolute Monarchy . . . by the Title of Creation. . . .

Thes. 26. God is the end, as well as the beginning of the divine Monarchy of the world. . . .

Thes. 28. All men as men are the subjects of God's Kingdom, as to Obligations and Duty, and God will not ask the consent of any man to be so obliged. . . .

Thes. 46. A Common-wealth properly so-called is . . . the Government of a Society of God's Subjects by a Sovereign subordinate to God, for the common good, and the Glory, and pleasing of God. . . .

Thes. 58. That is the best form of Government to this or that people, that all things considered, doth most powerfully tend to their spiritual and everlasting welfare, and their Holiness, Obedience, and pleasing of God. . . .

Thes. 74. Of all the three ordinary forms of Government, Democracy is to most people, and usually the worst. . . .

Thes. 192. The more Theocratical, or truly Divine any Government is, the better it is. . . .

Thes. 204. In a Divine Common-wealth, Holiness must have the principal honour and encouragement, and a great difference be made between the precious and the vile. . . .

Thes. 205. By this it appeareth that in a true Theocracy, or Divine Common-wealth, the Matter of the Church and Common-wealth should be altogether or almost the same, though the form of them and administrations are different. . . .

Thes. 214. The Moral Qualifications of Electors must be this, that no man choose but those that have publicly owned the Baptismal Covenant, personally, deliberately and seriously, taking the Lord for their only God, even the Father, Son and Holy Ghost, the Creator, Redeemer, and Sanctifier; and that lyeth not under the guilt of any of those sins for which God would have men put to death or cut off from his people . . . viz., for Blasphemy, Idolatry, persuading to Idolatry, Murder, Manstealing, Incest, Sodomy, Adultery, presumptuous sinning, and obstinate refusing to obey Magistrate, Priest, or Parent, in case of Gluttony, Drunkenness, and the like: and all such as would not seek the Lord: all wizzards, and that turn after wizzards, and more such like, which may easily be collected.

Thes. 206. It is this Theocratical Policy or Divine Common-wealth, which is the unquestionable reign of Christ on earth, which all Christians are agreed may be justly sought; and that temporal dignity of Saints, which undoubtedly would much bless the world."

All this was obviously fantastic in England. The British Commonwealth was after all British, not holy, even under Cromwell, and only a Puritan Roundhead could ever have hoped to turn it into a City of God. Even Baxter discovered his folly before he had finished the book. On April 25, 1659, he wrote: "When I had gone thus far, and was about to proceed a little further, the sudden News of the Armies Representation, and of the dissolving of the Parliament, and of the displeasure against my Book against Popery, called, *A Key for Catholicks,* and some other passages, interrupted me, and cast me upon these Meditations and Lamentations following. . . . I see more and more, how impossible it is, that honest, plain, and faithful dealing, in Ministers or others, should ordinarily find acceptance in the world! We must expect to displease God or men. . . . My God! I am satisfied! May I please thee, I have enough. . . . *Not my will, but thy will be done."* [3]

Thus ended the Holy Commonwealth in England. But in New England the case was quite different. What was sheer fantasy in England appeared to be a practical and literal reality in New England, for here the clergy were, as a matter of fact, the first citizens and leading spirits; here the social and political life centered about the various settlements and these settlements were organized into congregations. The magistrates were usually little more than sheriffs in the hands of the clergy. There was general agreement, at least in the first few decades, on fundamental religious and moral matters. The Puritan ideal, as Baxter described it above, was in New England more than an ideal; it was the professed rule of practice. Here the Holy Commonwealth seemed actually to have been established, and Baxter's treatise became almost a written constitution.

But even in New England the conception of the Holy Commonwealth was only gradually built up, and became generally accepted only as the course of events

[3] Baxter, pp. 491, 512, 513, 517.

seemed to favor it. Its foundations are usually attributed to Calvin, and it is true, Calvin was primarily responsible for formulating the fundamental political ideas of the English Puritans, but the theory which is distinctive of New England theocratic thought has little to do immediately with Calvin; in fact, it was developed in opposition to Presbyterian as well as to Anglican theories of church government. The basis for the Congregational theory is to be found in Doctor William Ames, Robert Parker, and the Parisian School.[4] Parker, in his *De Politeia Ecclesiastica Christi et Hierarchia opposita libri tres,* published in Holland in 1616, maintained that "the visible church instituted by Christ and his Apostles to which the keys are given, is not a Diocesan or Provincial or National Assembly but a particular congregation." [5] John Cotton's *The Keys of the Kingdom of Heaven* popularized this doctrine in New England, and when Rutherford replied by a defense of Presbyterian government, Thomas Hooker of Hartford wrote, in 1645, his famous *Survey of the Summe of Church Discipline,* "wherein the Way of the Congregational Churches of Christ in New England is warranted and all exceptions of weight made against it by sundry learned divines . . . are fully answered. Whereby it will appear to the judicious reader, that something more must be said than yet hath been, before their Principles can be shaken,

[4] See John Cotton: *The Way of Congregational Churches Cleared* (London, 1648), Pt. II, p. 23.

[5] *Cf.* Thomas Lechford: *Plain Dealing, or News from New England* (London, 1642), pp. 79-80 of the 1867 edition.

or they unsettled in their practice." These treatises, together with the Cambridge Platform adopted by the Synod of 1648, became the authoritative expositions of the theory in New England.

In these writings three covenants are discussed, all three of them in theory quite distinct but in practice closely allied: the Covenant of Grace, the Church Covenant, and the Civil Covenant. The Covenant of Grace is the invisible church of saints by calling, the whole body of God's elect. They are united to Christ, their head, by spiritual ties, by faith, and by the free grace of God, whereby they are justified and sanctified. God only knows infallibly who are saints and who not. The Church Covenant, or visible church, is a visible political union of saints. It is the duty of every saint to join a church, for, as Hooker put it, though the saints constitute the *matter* of Christ's Kingdom, its *form* is only by mutual covenant.[6] It was consequently necessary to set up some practical and human basis for segregating saints and sinners. For purposes of Church Covenant, therefore, saints were "such as have not only attained the knowledge of the principles of Religion, and are free from gros and open scandals, but also do together with the profession of their faith and repentance, walk in blameless obedience to the word, so as that in charitable discretion they may be

---

6 "This *Form* is the *Visible Covenant,* agreement, or consent whereby they give up themselves unto the Lord, to the observing of the ordinances of Christ together in the same society, which is usually called the Church-Covenant; For we see not otherwise how members can have Church-power one over another mutually." *The Cambridge Platform,* Ch. IV, Par. 3.

accounted Saints by calling (though perhaps some or more of them be unsound, and hypocrites inwardly)." [7]

This, it was thought, was a fairly reliable criterion; accordingly the churches, in order to safeguard themselves against hypocrites and offensive and scandalous persons, made an elaborate and explicit statement of the experience of redeeming grace in their souls a prerequisite for all church members. The following description of this process by Lechford appears to be substantially true:

"When a man or woman commeth to joyne unto the Church so gathered, he or shee commeth to the Elders in private. . . . And if they satisfie the Elders, and the private assembly, . . . that they are true beleevers, that they have beene wounded in their hearts for their originall sinne, and actuall transgressions, and can pitch upon some promise of free grace in the Scripture, for the ground of their faith, and that they finde their hearts drawne to beleeve in Christ Jesus, for their justification and salvation, and these in the ministerie of the Word, reading or conference: and that they know competently the summe of Christian faith. And sometimes, though they be not come to a full assurance of their good estate in Christ. Then afterwards, in convenient time, in the publique assembly of the Church, . . . the Elder turneth his speech to the party to be admitted, and requireth him, or sometimes asketh him, if he be willing to make knowne to the congregation the work of grace upon his soule; and biddeth him, as

[7] *The Cambridge Platform*, Ch. III, Par. 1.

briefly, and audibly, to as good hearing as he can, to doe the same.

"Thereupon the party, if it be a man, speaketh himselfe; but if it be a woman, her confession made before the Elders, in private, is most usually (in Boston church) read by the Pastor, who registred the same. At Salem the women speake themselves, for the most part, in the Church; but of late it is said, they doe this upon the week dayes there, and nothing is done on Sunday, but their entrance into Covenant. The man in a solemne speech, sometimes a quarter of an houre long, shorter or longer, declareth the work of grace in his soule, to the same purpose, as that before the Elders formerly mentioned.

"Then the Elder requireth the party to make profession of his faith; which also is done either by questions and answers, if the party be weake, or else in a solemne speech according to the summe and tenour of the Christian faith laid downe in the Scriptures."[8]

This ordeal was regarded as a sufficient barrier to all who were not saints, and it certainly kept out of the church even many who were saints, but who disliked these many public professions and confessions.[9]

---

[8] Thomas Lechford: *Plain Dealing* (1867 edition), pp. 18-23.

[9] Concerning these, Cotton Mather comments: "The Jews tell us of . . . a Scare-Crow upon the top of the Temple, which kept off the fowls from defiling of it; and it hath been the Opinion of many that this Custom of Relations, to be made by Candidates for Admission to the Church, of what operations of the regenerating spirit have been upon their souls . . . is as a Scare-crow to keep men out of the Temple; but, it may be, it has been the Opinion of as many, that none but the Defilers of the Temple would be kept out by such a Scare-crow." Cotton Mather: *Magnalia Christi Americana* (London, 1702), Bk. V, Ch. XVII, "Historical Remarks," Sec. 6.

Those who remained outside of the Church Covenant, though they attended church regularly, were spoken of as the unregenerate, so that for all practical purposes the invisible and the visible churches came to be identified. Lechford states that "many good people scruple their Church Covenant, so highly tearmed by the most of them, a part of the Covenant of grace." [10] And no doubt this was the practical attitude of the churches, though in strict theory the two covenants were held to be separate. Hooker spoke of churches as "little kingdoms or cities of Christ," and Governor Bradford, speaking of the founding of the Plymouth church, said: "The Lords free people, joyned themselves (by a covenant of the Lord) into a church estate, in the felowship of the gospell." [11] The text of the Covenant of the church of Salem is also good evidence of the practical unity of the two covenants in the minds of the early settlers:

"We covenant with our Lord, and one with another; and we do bind ourselves in the presence of God, to walk together in all his ways, according as he is pleased to reveal himself unto us in his blessed word of truth; and do explicitly, in the name and fear of God, profess and protest to walk as followeth, through the power and grace of our Lord Jesus Christ. We avouch the Lord to be our God, and ourselves to be his people, in the truth and simplicity of our spirits. We resolve to approve ourselves to the Lord in our particular call-

[10] Lechford, pp. 56-7.
[11] William Bradford: *History of the Plymouth Plantation*, Ch. I. In Hart: *American History Told by Contemporaries*, Vol. I, p. 168.

ings; shunning idleness as the bane of any state; nor will we deal hardly or oppressingly with any, wherein we are the Lord's stewards. Promising also unto our best ability to teach our children, and servants the knowledge of God, and of His Will, that they may serve Him also; and all this not by any strength of our own, but by the Lord Christ: whose blood we desire may sprinkle this our Covenant made in His name."

Cotton Mather, who cites this covenant in his *Magnalia,* immediately adds, "By this instrument was the Covenant of Grace explained, received, and recognized, by the first Church in this Colony, and applied unto the evangelical designs of a Church-estate before the Lord." [12] This indicates that he, too, at a much later date, regarded the Church Covenant as a Covenant of Grace.

As to the third covenant, civil government, here again in theory church and state were distinct, but in practice not. Theoretically God set up ministers to declare his will and magistrates to execute it; ministers had authority to counsel, advise and admonish; magistrates to command, judge and punish. But in reality the civil compact was merely the physical enforcement and public advancement of whatever the churches desired. Religion was not a department or phase of social life; it was the end and aim of all life; and to it, consequently, all institutions were subordinated. *The Cambridge Platform* gives formal expression to this doctrine: "Church-government stands in no oppo-

[12] Mather: *Magnalia,* Bk. I, Ch. III, Sec. 6.

23

sition to civil government of common wealths, nor any intrencheth upon the authority of Civil Magistrates in their jurisdictions; . . . It is not in the power of Magistrates to compell their subjects to become church members, . . . As it is unlawful for church officers to meddle with the sword of the Magistrate, so it is unlawful for the Magistrate to meddle with the work proper to church-officers." [13]

Having made this distinction, the Platform immediately proceeds to obscure it as follows: "It is the duty of the Magistrate, to take care of matters of religion, and to improve his civil authority for the observing of the duties commanded in the second table. They are called God's. The end of the Magistrate's office, is not only the quiet and peaceable life of the subject, in matters of righteousness and honesty, but also in matters of godliness, yea of all godliness." [14]

Thus it is evident that in practice, and to a large extent even in theory, the three covenants were really one. The Church Covenant gave form to the Cove-

---

[13] *The Cambridge Platform*, Ch. XVII, Secs. 2, 4, 5.

[14] "The object of the power of the Magistrate, are not things meerly inward, and so not subject to his cognisance and view, as unbeleife, hardness of heart, erronious opinions not vented; but only such things as are acted by the outward man; neither is their power to be exercised, in commanding such acts of the outward man, and punishing the neglect thereof, as are but meer inventions, and devices of men; but about such acts, as are commanded and forbidden in the word; yea such as the word doth clearly determine, though not alwayes clearly to the judgment of the Magistrate or others, yet clearly in itselfe. In these he of right ought to putt forth his authority, though oft-times actually he doth it not. Idolatry, Blasphemy, Heresy, venting corrupt and pernicious opinions, that destroy the foundation, open contempt of the word preached, prophanation of the Lord's Day, disturbing the peaceable administration and exercise of the worship and holy things of God, and the like, are to be restrayned, and punished by civil authority." *The Cambridge Platform*, Ch. XVII, Secs. 6, 7, 8.

nant of Grace, and the Civil Covenant gave power to the Church Covenant. Society in New England was actually organized, as Baxter said it should be, into a Holy Commonwealth.

In fact, while Baxter was writing his treatise in England, the Reverend John Eliot, of Roxbury, Massachusetts, was writing his *Christian Commonwealth: or, The Civil Polity of the Rising Kingdom of Jesus Christ,* which was the most radical treatise of all. He advocated a system of unified administration, modelled on the scriptural system of the ancient Israelites, under God, the supreme king.[15]

The details of Eliot's scheme of government were quite impractical, and even had the Restoration not caused him, at the order of the General Court of Massachusetts, to suppress his book because he had said harsh words about all earthly kings, it would scarcely have become the practical guide that Baxter's

---

[15] According to him the substance of the covenant by which a people subject themselves unto the Lord, to be ruled by him in all things, is this: "That they do humbly confess their corruption by nature, and lost condition; that they acknowledge the free grace of God, in their redemption by Christ, and in the promulgation of the Gospel unto them, and making application thereof effectually unto their souls: and therefore the Lord hath shewed his everlasting Love unto them, and caused them inwardly by faith, to give up themselves, unto him, to be forever his, to love, serve, and obey him, in all his Word and Commandments: so now, they do outwardly, and solemnly with the rest of God's people joyn together so to do in their Civil Polity, receiving from the Lord both the platform of their Civil Government, as it is set down (in the essentials of it) in the holy Scriptures; and also their Laws, which they resolve through his grace, to fetch out of the Word of God making that their only Magna Charta; and accounting no Law, Statute or Judgement valid, farther than it appeareth to arise and flow from the Word of God." John Eliot: *The Christian Commonwealth* (London, 1660), Ch. I, Par. 2. In *Massachusetts Historical Collections,* Third Series, Vol. IX, pp. 143-4.

was. Nevertheless his general theory was quite typical and expressed the basic ideas of Puritan thought.

The appeal to Biblical authority was a consequence, rather than a cause, of these ideas. To be sure, the Puritans were in the habit of calling their convictions Biblical just as we call ours scientific, but this was little more than an official sanction or divine rubber-stamp. The Bible, no less than science, is sufficiently flexible to sanction whatever it is supposed to sanction. The Puritans, searching the Scriptures for texts relevant to their own particular needs, soon discovered the general similarity between themselves and the ancient Israelites. The Lord had obviously chosen them, as he had the children of Israel, to carry out his plans for the redemption of the world. They had been driven from their homes into a wilderness, not out of punishment, but for the sake of building a promised land. The chief difference between them and the ancient Hebrews, as they saw it, was that they were called upon to make a promised land out of the very wilderness itself. It would be difficult to understand how a tradition as foreign as the Hebraic account of history could be so firmly implanted in American soil, had it not possessed an initial relevancy and moral vitality. The Puritans' constant preoccupation with the Old Testament and the Mosaic law was not merely a consequence of their belief in the authority of sacred scriptures; it was rather the natural turning for comfort and counsel to a people who seemed to have undergone a similar experience. They turned to Jewish law, as they

did to their English common law, as a definite working basis and precedent for their own institutions,
preference being given usually to the Mosaic code
where it was at all workable, since it was constructed
on a theocratic basis and adapted to the wilderness.
Only the remoteness in time and space of the ancient
Israelites, and the consequent cultural difficulties in
applying the Mosaic law, prevented Puritan law from
becoming more Jewish and less English than it actually
turned out to be. But even when their actual laws
were quite thoroughly English, the sanction which attached to them was frequently that of the Law of the
Lord, together with the confidence and awe which that
Law inspired. Not only their laws but all their institutions were thus given a sanctity which only a Biblical commonwealth could command, and there pre-
vailed a general confidence in the success of their adventure which a less historical philosophy could hardly
have engendered. The belief in their divine election
for a great work soon ceased to be a mere faith and
came to be regarded as an empirical fact. Accordingly,
when Baxter's treatise was imported into New England, it was immediately recognized as a complete exposition of what New England professed to be, and it
merely remained for the clergy to expound and celebrate the grand doctrine.

This idea of the Holy Commonwealth made it easy
for the Puritans to bring their philosophy of history
up to date. God was evidently merely completing the

work which he began in the Reformation.[16] Of the three traditional offices of the Savior, Hooker tells us [17] the prophetical office had been established by the early reformers, the priestly office by Luther; it remained for Christ to establish his kingly office, the office which Anti-Christ had most successfully obstructed.

"These are the times drawing on, wherein prophecies are to attain their performances: . . . These are the times, when the knowledge of the Lord shall cover the earth as the waters the sea; . . . These are the times when people shall be fitted for such privileges, fit I say to obtain them, and fit to use them. . . . Now the Lord will write his laws in their hearts, and put it into their inward parts, and they shall teach no more every man his neighbour, for they shall all know me, from the least of them, to the greatest of them. . . . This being the season, when all the kingdoms of the world, are becoming the Lord's and his Christ's; and to this purpose he is taking to himself his great might, which heretofore he seemed to lay aside. . . . This present term of God's patience promiseth some allowance to his people, . . . to take leave, to lay claim to the priviledges, which they have conceived to be part of the legacy bequeathed unto them by the Lord Jesus, being estated and entitled members of the visible Kingdome of his Church."

This proclamation of the coming of the Kingdom of

[16] John Cotton's sermon, *The Churches' Resurrection* (printed in London, 1642), is an excellent presentation of this theory.

[17] Preface to his *Survey of the Summe of Church Discipline* (London, 1648).

Christ was in effect a declaration of independence of
all earthly authority. Theocracy was, humanly speaking, synonymous with the democracy of the elect; and
this democracy, if we may take the above passage
from Hooker seriously, was expected to lead soon to
a holy anarchy, when men will obey the laws of God
written in their hearts and "they shall teach no more
every man his neighbour." This was the essence of
Christian liberty, the liberty to be subject only to
Christ. Samuel Mather, in his *Apology for the Liberties of the Churches in New England,* called it the
liberty of the laity. The keys of the Kingdom were
in the hands of the members of particular congregations. Hitherto the keys of the Kingdom had been
passed on, supposedly from Christ to his Apostles, from
Apostles to popes, from popes to prelates, and from
prelates to priests. Even in the Protestant churches,
ministers were ordained *von oben herab,* with much
ceremony and under the pomp and display of a hierarchy of authority. Imagine, then, the thrill, or even
the shudder, which must have passed through those
who took part in the following scene, described by
Charles Gott, of Salem, in a letter to Governor Bradford of Plymouth:

"The 20th of July, it pleased the Lord to move the
heart of our Governor to set it apart for a solemn day
of humiliation, for the choice of a pastor and teacher.
. . . (Their choice was after this manner: every fit
member wrote, in a note, his name whom the Lord
moved him to think was fit for a pastor, and so like-

wise, whom they would have for teacher; so the most voice was for Mr. Skelton to be Pastor, and Mr. Higginson to be Teacher;) So Mr. Skelton was chosen pastor and Mr. Higginson to be teacher; and they accepting the choice, Mr. Higginson, with three or four of the gravest members of the Church, laid their hands on Mr. Skelton, using prayer therewith. This being done, there was imposission of hands on Mr. Higginson also. (Then there was proceeding in election of elders and deacons, but they were only named, and laying on of hands deferred, to see if it pleased God to send us more able men over.)" [18]

The sacred office of imposition of hands, which for centuries had been the exclusive privilege of popes and bishops, was here performed by a few pioneer farmers. No wonder some looked upon it as a most monstrous sacrilege, and others as an exhibition of the wonder-working Providence in New England. Literally, *vox populi* was *vox dei*. Prometheus himself, when he stole Jove's fire, showed no more daring in the face of God than these simple, grave farmers, when they themselves selected and ordained their ministers, "called of God." In fact, the theocracy was, from the point of view of the elect, both in theory and practice an assertion of liberty and democracy. From the point of view of the unregenerate, of course, this monarchy of God was the most thorough-going tyranny imaginable; but with the unregenerate we are not now concerned,

[18] Quoted in Williston Walker: *The Creeds and Platforms of Congregationalism* (New York, 1893), pp. 103-4.

for this philosophy was first of all a philosophy of the elect, erected for their own liberty, enlightenment and consolation, and only later became a halo for overawing the unregenerate.

Nothing seemed more evident to the minds of the Puritans than that God was actually taking a hand in establishing his kingdom on earth. "The God of Heaven had carried a nation into a wilderness upon the designs of a glorious reformation." [19]

The whole meaning and purpose of these events burst upon their imagination. It was God who had elected them by his sovereign grace and to his own glory; it was God who had sent them into the howling wilderness; and it was God's glory and Christ's kingship that was being manifested in them. [20]

And Cotton Mather, whose *Magnalia Christi Americana* represents the culmination and classic expression

---

[19] Mather: *Magnalia*, Bk. III, Sec. 1.

[20] "It hath been deservedly esteemed one of the great and wonderful works of God in this last age, that the Lord stirred up the spirits of so many thousands of his servants, to leave the pleasant land of England, the land of their nativity, and to transport themselves, and families, over the ocean sea, into a desert land in America, at the distance of a thousand leagues from their own country; and this, meerly on the account of pure and undefiled religion, not knowing how they should have their daily bread, but trusting in God for that, in the way of seeking first the kingdom of God, and the righteousness thereof: And that the Lord was pleased to grant such a gracious presence of his with them, and such a blessing upon their undertakings, that within a few years a wilderness was subdued before them. . . . Surely of this work and of this time, it shall be said, what hath God wrought? And, this is the Lord's doings, it is marvellous in our eyes! Even so (O Lord) didst thou lead thy people, to make thyself a glorious name! . . . For the Lord our God hath in his infinite wisdom, grace, and holiness, contrived and established His covenant, so as he will be the God of his people, and of their seed with them, and after them, in their generations; and in the ministerial dispensation of the covenant of grace, in, with and to his visible church." John Higginson: Preface to Cotton Mather's *Magnalia Christi Americana*.

of this philosophy, ventured to prophesy: " 'Tis possible, that our Lord Jesus Christ carried some thousands of Reformers into the retirements of an American desart, on purpose, that, with an opportunity granted unto many of his faithful servants, to enjoy the precious liberty of their ministry, though in the midst of many temptations all their days, He might there, to them first, and then by them, give a specimen of many good things, which He would have His Churches elsewhere aspire and arise unto: and this being done, he knows not whether there be not all done, that New England was planted for; and whether the Plantation may not, soon after this, come to nothing." [21]

All this seemed to the Puritan thinkers so clear that, as Cotton Mather said, " 'tis nothing but Atheism in the hearts of men, that can persuade them otherwise." [22]   And they believed in it as a thing of which they were eye-witnesses.   In fact, Cotton Mather describes the leaders of New England as actors in a divine drama.   God, they imagined, had elected them from all eternity to play just this rôle, and the assurance of their election and of the dignity and importance of their parts led to such acting as has seldom been seen on the stage of history—such exuberance and whole-hearted devotion at the first, and then, as their rôle became apparently more tragic, such heroic intensity and strutting pride—surely none but a supernatural explanation can do it justice!

[21] *Magnalia,* General Introduction, Par. 3.
[22] *Ibid.,* Par. 4.

Nor was this philosophy merely a rhetorical device by which the ministers embellished their sermons; it seems to have pervaded the daily actions of common people. Here, for instance, is a piece of pious exultation on the part of an ordinary sea captain:

"It was God that did draw me by his Providence out of my Father's family, and weaned me from it by degrees; It was God put into my heart to incline to live abroad; and it was God that made my Father willing. God by His Providence brought me near Mr. Warham, and inclined my heart to his Ministry, God by his Providence moved the Heart of my Master Mossiour to ask me whether I would go to New England: It was God by his Providence that made me willing to leave my dear Father, and dear brethren and sisters, my dear friends and Country: It was God that made my Father willing upon the first motion I made in person, to let me go: It was God that sent Mr. Maverick that pious Minister to me, who was unknown to him, to seek me out that I might come hither. So God brought me out of Plymouth the 20th of March in the Year, 1629, 30, and landed me in health at Nantasket, on the 30th of May—1630, I being then about the age of twenty-one years. Blessed be God that brought me here!" [23]

Evidently the philosophy of God's sovereignty and of divine predestination afforded no small comfort and stimulus to these early settlers. Many an Ameri-

---

[23] Captain Roger Clap: *Memoirs* (Boston, 1731). In Hart: *American History Told by Contemporaries,* Vol. I, p. 196.

can colony had started under more favorable auspices than those of New England and had suffered collapse. Even an optimistic sociologist would probably have predicted failure for the pilgrims. With little support from the mother country, and no material resources of their own, they faced a severe climate and a howling wilderness. How much the consciousness that they were not ultimately responsible, that they were being led by a greater power, had to do with their success is difficult to tell. It has no doubt been exaggerated by past historians and is probably underestimated by those of today. Certainly it is little short of a miracle of human discipline and energy that in the face of circumstances that would have baffled and ruined most adventurers, these Puritans not only made themselves physically secure, but in addition began immediately to lay the foundations of government, education, thought and literature which, though provincial, yet far outshone the achievements of any other colony, and made New England the intellectual leader of the nation. New England, of course, as even New Englanders now admit, turned out to be anything but holy; nevertheless, it is quite possible that, but for the idea of the Holy Commonwealth, the Commonwealth of Massachusetts would not have been established. However that may be, the case of New England is, at least, a significant proof that the doctrine that man is not a free agent, that he is merely an actor in a cosmic drama, playing a predetermined rôle, may be a more powerful stimulus to extreme effort and a more moral

34

force than any doctrine of human freedom. It is one of the ironies of history that William James, with New England all about him, should have believed that the reserve energies of man could not be tapped by a deterministic philosophy.

CHAPTER II

THE WARS OF THE LORD

"If anyone would draw the picture of the church (saith Luther) let him take a silly poor maid, sitting in a wilderness, compassed about with hungry lions, wolves, boars and bears, and all manner of cruel and hurtful beasts; and in the midst of many furious men assaulting her every moment: for this is her condition in the world. Behold that picture of the Church exemplified in the story of New England, . . . the people of the Lord Jesus Christ, led into the wilderness of New England, have not only met with a continual temptation of the devil there; the wilderness having always had serpents in it; but also they have had in almost every new lustre of years, a new assault of extraordinary temptation upon them; a more than common hour and power of darkness." [1]

Plato claimed that before his Republic could be established the adult population must be killed off. The Holy Commonwealth proved to be no less preposterous. Obstacles immediately beset it and rapidly grew so alarming to the champions of the Lord, that they supposed the devil himself had taken notice of

[1] Cotton Mather: *Magnalia Christi Americana* (London, 1702), Bk. VII, Intro. and Ch. I, Par. 1.

36

New England's cosmic significance and had bent all his efforts to its undoing. Being regarded as a phase of the universal conflict with evil, the ensuing struggles were not hindrances to the acceptance of the Puritan ideal; far from being grounds for doubt, they were signals for redoubled effort. An hypothesis can be tested, but a faith must be fought. The faith in the Holy Commonwealth, at least, could not possibly be refuted. It finally died, but it never was disproved. To be sure, the early dream that the Kingdom of Christ was at last established in purity and tranquillity soon proved to be false, as New England became merely one more battlefield for the church militant. But this disillusion came quickly and the Puritans accepted the challenge willingly, even eagerly, being from the start an aggressive and militant party. They soon became accustomed to the conviction that the more New England prospered, the more it would be attacked by the devil and his agents. Or, as the Antinomians put it, "the darker our sanctification is, the clearer is our justification." [2] Consequently, the more desperate the fortunes of the Holy Commonwealth became, the more stubbornly its champions waged what Cotton Mather called the wars of the Lord. Under such circumstances the idea of the Holy Commonwealth was transformed from a gospel of comfort and encouragement for a poor people in the

[2] Cited in C. F. Adams: *The Antinomian Controversy* (Boston, 1892), pp. 162-3.

wilderness, into a weapon of warfare in the hands of an elect minority.

Not long after the founding of Massachusetts Bay, the devil, it seems, conceived the idea of entering the Indians for the purpose of harassing the rising Kingdom of Christ. The Lord, foreseeing this, had in his kind providence sent a pestilence among them just prior to the landing of the Pilgrims, which had killed off great numbers, so that, according to the story, the woods were full of dead Indians when the Pilgrims landed. (The same pestilence attacked the Pilgrims too, though of course for another reason!) But in spite of this divine precaution, the Indians soon became troublesome.

It must be remembered that in England merchant adventurers, in order to get the necessary Christian capital, made it a practice to promise stockholders that their colonists would be actively engaged in converting the heathen natives; and it was only on the strength of this plea that many of the prominent middle-class Puritans had been persuaded to invest money in such doubtful business enterprises. Therefore, when the early New England settlements proved to be financial failures (from the investor's point of view) the colonists were charged with maladministration of the company's business. Among other matters it was suggested that the colonists give more thought to the conversion of the heathen and less to their own holy commonwealths. The colonists replied that many Indians attended their worship, that not a few had been converted, and that John Eliot was actively engaged in preaching to them in their own language. However, John Eliot was merely the exception that proved the rule. In general the New Englanders took the attitude that the Indians were not fit subjects for their Kingdom of God, and to support this point of view they had much evidence which the missionary enthusiasts at home could not appreciate. John Cotton even found a passage in the Scriptures indicating that it was not the will of God that the Indians should be converted until certain other things had first taken place.

"There may be doubt that for a time there will be no great hope of any national conversion, till Antichrist be ruined, and the Jews converted; because the Church of God is said to be filled with smoke, till the seven plagues (which are to be poured upon the Antichristian state) be fulfilled: And till then, no man (that is, no considerable number of men out of the Church, as Pagans be) shall be able to enter into the Church, *Rev.* 15, 8. Yet nevertheless, that hindreth not, but that some sprinklings, and gleanings of them may be brought home to Christ." [3]

Coming to more empirical arguments, he cited an experience of the Catholics in Maryland: "I received advertisement from Mr. James (one of the ministers, who went to Virginia upon the Lord's worke, of which I spake before) that whilst he was detained (by winds) in Maryland (a Popish Plantation between us and Vir-

---

[3] John Cotton: *The Way of Congregational Churches Cleared* (London, 1648), Pt. I, p. 78. Reprinted with Hooker's *Summe of Church Discipline*.

ginia) he saw, as I remember, (for his Letter is not present at hand with me) 40 Indians baptized in new shirts, which the Catholicks had given them for their incouragement unto Baptisme. But he tarried there so long for a faire winde, that before his departure, he saw the Indians (when their shirts were foule, and they knew not how to wash them) come againe to make a new motion, either the Catholick English there must give them new shirts, or else they would renounce their Baptisme." [4]

After a few Indian disturbances the Puritans not only generally accepted this point of view, but even regarded the savages as clearly direct instruments of Satan. And later, when it was found that the French and Indians were cooperating, the latter were doubly hated, as not only in the service of the devil, but of Anti-Christ, too. There was no hesitation in battling for the Lord. Even Thomas Shepard, first minister of Cambridge, and one of the gentler spirits, describes the massacre of the Pequots as follows: ". . . the second night the Providence of God guided them to another nearer [fort], full of stout men and there brot soldiers, being as it were coopt up there, to the number of three or four hundred in all for the divine slaughter by the hand of the English. These therefore being all night making merry and singing the death of the English the next day. . . . The English being come to it awakened the fort with a peale of muskets, directed into the midst of their wigwams, and after this, some under-

---

[4] John Cotton: *The Way of Congregational Churches Cleared* (London, 1648), Pt. I, p. 80.

taking to compasse the fort without, some adventured into the fort upon the very faces of the enemy standing ready with their arrows ready bent to shoot whoever should adventure, but the English casting by their peeces, took their swords in their hands (the Lord doubling their strength and courage) and fell upon the Indians, where a hot fight continued about the space of an houre, at last by the direction of one Captayne Mason their wigwams were set on fire as being dry and contiguous one to another was right dreadfull to the Indians, some burning, some bleeding to death by the sword, some resisting till they were cut off, some flying were beat down by the men without, until the Lord had utterly consumed the whole company except four or five girles they tooke prisoners, and dealt with them at Seabrooke as they dealt with ours at Wethersfield, and tis verily thought scarce one man escaped unless one or two to carry forth tydings of the lamentable end of their fellowes; and of the English not one man was killed, but one by the musket of an Englishman (as was conceived), some were wounded much, but all recovered and restored agayne." [5]

The devil, being thus routed by the divine slaughter in the hands of the English, soon bethought himself of other methods of attack, and consequently many of the most pious people in New England found themselves strangely persecuted by witches. Witches were, of course, a common fact in Europe, and it was not surprising that they should make their appearance in

[5] Thomas Shepard: *Autobiography* (Boston, 1832), pp. 62, 63.

New England; but the peculiarly intimate and important relationship between the Puritans and the powers that govern the world made witches and similar wonders of the invisible world exceptionally serious in New England.[6]

It is not necessary to relate here the familiar story of the witchcraft scare during the last decade of the seventeenth century, centering in Salem, and dominating the imagination of all New England; but it is important to describe the general quality of the Puritan imagination of which this was merely a symptom, and to show how the same mental trait produced both the witchcraft scare and the Great Awakening.

To one who is accustomed to think of each event as the direct handiwork of God and who understands it only when he can relate it to the economy of redemption, the study of nature is necessarily a moral and teleological inquiry. What we call natural science was not so much something which the Puritans were afraid of and shunned as dangerous to their faith, as it was something entirely irrelevant to their interests and problems. Nature was instructive to them only in so far as it suggested the hidden mysterious operations of designing agents. God and devil were both active, scheming, hidden powers, each pursuing his own ends by various ministrations, and natural events were there-

---

[6] The epidemic of witchcraft has been generally attributed to the Puritan régime, but it has now been proved quite conclusively that the Puritans were not exceptional in this matter. What happened in New England was merely typical of a general phenomenon in European countries. It is significant not as an effect of Puritanism, but for its effects upon the Puritan theology. See the bibliography for Chapter II at the end of this book.

fore to be understood only in so far as they showed evidence of some divine or diabolical plot. From this point of view there was in New England no small interest in natural phenomena. In 1681 the ministers of Massachusetts made some proposals concerning the recording of illustrious providences. "Such Divine judgments, tempests, floods, earthquakes, thunders as are unusual, strange apparitions, or whatever else shall happen that is prodigious, witchcrafts, diabolical possessions, remarkable judgements upon noted sinners, eminent deliverances, and answers of prayer, are to be reckoned among illustrious providences." Increase Mather's volume of *Remarkable Providences* was the outcome. One specimen will suffice to indicate its general character. At the end of the chapter entitled "Philosophical Meditations," a chapter devoted to observations upon electrical and magnetic phenomena, there occurs the story of how a "prophane man" was converted during a fearful thunder-storm, by the pious calm of a Puritan woman, and the author concludes: "This was an happy thunder-storm." [7]

Cotton Mather continued his father's scientific investigations and published them in a little volume entitled *The Christian Philosopher, a Collection of the best discoveries in nature with religious improvements*.[8] A few selections from it may serve to put the reader into the proper frame of mind for studying nature: "Of

[7] Increase Mather: *Remarkable Providences* (London, 1890), pp. 94-5.
[8] Sub-title: "Religio Philosophica, or, the Christian Philosopher: being A Commentary, of the more Modern and Certain Philosophy, upon that Instruction, Job XXXVI, 24. *Remember that thou magnify His work which Men behold.*" (London, 1721.)

the Sun. A most Glorious and most Useful Creature! But still a creature! By Old Astronomers call'd, *Cor Planetarum*. There will be no Athenians now to araign me for it, if I call it, The Carbuncle of the Heavens. Kircher supposes the Sun to be a Body of wondrous Fire, unequal in surface, composed of Parts which are of a different Nature, some Fluid, some solid: the Disque of it, a Sea of Fire, wherein Waves of astonishing Flame have a perpetual agitation.

"Sir Isaac Newton, as well as Dr. Hook, takes the Sun to be a solid and opake Body. Dr. Hook thinks this Body to be encompassed with a vast Atmosphere, the Shell whereof is all that shines. The Light of the Sun he takes to be from the Burning of the more superficial Parts, which are set on fire, which may be without hazard of being burnt out in a vast Number of Ages. And Sir Isaac Newton thinks the Sun to be a sort of a mighty Earth, most vehemently hot; the Heat whereof is conserved by the marvellous Bigness of the Body." [9]

"Glorious God, thou art the Father of Lights, the Maker of the Sun! . . . Enjoying the Benefits of the Sun, I will glorify him that made it: Thou alone art forever to be adored, O thou Maker of that Glorious Creature! . . . How glorious will the Righteous be in that World, when they shall shine as the Sun?" [10] . . .

"Dr. Cheyne observes, If our Moon were bigger, or nearer the Earth, or if we had more than one, we

[9] Cotton Mather: *The Christian Philosopher*, pp. 25-6.
[10] *Ibid.*, pp. 30-1.

should be every now and then in hazard of being drowned. And if our present Moon were less, or at a greater distance, or if there were none at all, we should be in hazard of being stifled with the baneful steams of a stagnating Ocean. It is evident our Satellit is most wisely contrived for our Purposes,—by thee, O our Gracious God!" [11] . . .

"Of the Vegetables. The Contrivance of our most Glorious Creator, in the Vegetables growing upon this Globe, cannot be wisely observed without Admiration and Astonishment. We will single out some Remarkables, and glorify our God!" [12] . . .

"A great Philosopher observes and affirms, that the Clearness of our Fancy depends on the regular structure of the Brain; by which it is fitted for the receiving and compounding of all Impressions with the more Regularity. In Fools the Brain is deformed. The Deformity is not easily noted in other People: But, no doubt, a smaller Difference than can be imagined, may alter the Symmetry of the Brain, and so the Perspicuity of the Fancy.

"Gracious God! how much ought I to adore the Goodness of thy superintending Providence, which gave my Brain that Conformation, that enables me now to see and write thy praises.

"The Head has wonderful things to show: But can any thing in the World be shown so curious and marvellous as the Eye! Our excellent Ray says truly, Not the least Curiosity can be added to it. What

[11] *Ibid.*, p. 50.   [12] *Ibid.*, p. 122.

Rhetorick, what Poetry can sufficiently celebrate the Glories of this admirable Organ! How perverted the Eye, which is not ever unto the Lord, the glorious Maker of it!" [13] . . .

"The Union between the Soul and the Body is altogether inexplicable, the Soul not having any Surface to touch the Body, and the Body not having any Sentiment as the Soul. The Union of the Soul and Body does consist, . . . in the conformity of our Thoughts to our Corporeal Actions; but, for the Explication of this Conformity we must have recourse to a Superior Power. Truly, Sirs, do what you can, you must quickly come to that!" [14]

"Hear now the Conclusion of the Matter. To enkindle the Dispositions and the Resolutions of Piety in my Brethren, is the Intention of all my Essays, and must be the Conclusion of them.

"Atheism is now for ever chased and hissed out of the World, every thing in the World concurs to a Sentence of Banishment upon it. Fly, thou Monster, and hide, and let not the darkest recesses of Africa itself be able to cherish thee; never dare to shew thyself in a World where every thing stands ready to overwhelm thee! A Being that must be superior to Matter, even the Creator and Governor of all Matter, is every where so conspicuous, that there can be nothing more monstrous than to deny the God that is above." [15]

Here the interest is evidently teleological; the knowl-

---

[13] Cotton Mather: *The Christian Philosopher*, pp. 234-5.
[14] *Ibid.*, p. 291.
[15] *Ibid.*, p. 294.

edge of nature is not an end in itself, it is valued for
its religious improvements. It would have been as idle
to ask the Puritan to experiment on the causes of light-
ning as it would have been to ask Franklin to make
religious improvements on his discoveries. Scientific
knowledge was for the Puritan merely a matter of
philosophic curiosity, not an inherently significant
enterprise of the mind, and it was consequently valued
for its incidental contributions to what the Puritan regarded as the prime goal of all knowledge—the glorification of God. The Puritan, like Socrates, was quite
content to allow the physical cause of an event to
remain mysterious, or even miraculous, provided he
had some idea of its final cause; and, conversely, the
natural scientist is quite content to allow the goal to
remain mysterious, provided the details of its operation
are made explicit. These two types of knowledge are
ideally supplementary, but historically they have seldom cooperated. The moralist and the scientist usually irritate each other. In our own day we have generally abandoned the search for the *final* causes of
nature, because we have no confidence in our ability
to construct a reliable technique of verification in these
matters; the Puritans, on the other hand, abandoned
the search for *physical* causes for precisely the same
reason. They regarded natural philosophy as a matter
of sheer speculation, whereas the pursuit of the knowledge of God and his ways seemed to them an empirical
and hopeful undertaking. They were convinced they
had evidence of *why* God did what he did, but to ask

how he did it was thought to be vain and perhaps even impertinent curiosity.

What is true of natural science is true of the other secular realms of the imagination. The fine arts were cultivated only in so far as they seemed to have a bearing on the economy of redemption; accordingly there flourished chiefly the arts of oratory and argument. Secular arts, learning and education were regarded as luxuries, unnecessary for the greater glory of God and the propagation of his Gospel. New England was supposed to be dedicated to a single task, and this unified aim naturally dominated its mental trends even more thoroughly than its physical pursuits. In short the mind of the Puritan was singularly unified and his imagination thoroughly moralized. The clergy were, of course, the professional moral scientists, but the laymen were no less dominated by such mental habits. The common man and illiterate shared with the expert this interest in divining God's purposes in the course of events. No event was merely natural; it was an act of God and was hence surcharged with that "numinous" quality which gives birth to both prophetic insight and mystic illumination.

With this moralized imagination he now approached the problem of witchcraft. He asked, first and last, why should there be witches here? The devil, was the obvious reply. Why should the devil plague us? Again the answer was old and obvious: why *shouldn't* the devil plague the

Lord's elect? [16] The witches and other preternatural occurrences thus easily fitted into the philosophy of the wars of the Lord, and as time went on the Puritans began to expect the unexpected, to accept the preternatural as empirical evidence of diabolical afflictions. Cotton Mather records the following incident in the life of Anne Hutchinson:

"The erroneous gentlewoman herself, convicted of holding about thirty monstrous opinions, growing big with child, and at length coming to her time of travail, was delivered of about thirty monstrous birth at once; whereof some were bigger and some were lesser; of several figures; few of any perfect, none of any Humane shape. This was a thing generally then asserted and believed; whereas by some that were eyewitnesses, it is affirmed, that these were no more monstrous births, than what it is frequent for women, labouring with false conceptions, to produce. Moreover, one very nearly related unto this gentlewoman, and infected with her herisies, was on October 17, 1637, delivered of as hideous a monster as perhaps the sun ever lookt upon. It had no head: the face was below

[16] "There has been too much cause to observe, that the christians who were driven into the American desart, which is now call'd New England, have to their sorrow seen Azazel dwelling and raging there in very tragical instances. The devils have doubtless felt a more than ordinary vexation, from the arrival of those christians with their sacred exercises of christianity in this wilderness: But the sovereignty of heaven has permitted them still to remain in the wilderness for our vexation, as well as their own. Molestations from evil spirits, in more sensible and surprising operations, than those finer methods, wherein they commonly work upon the minds of all men, but especially of ill men, have so abounded in this country, that I question whether any one town has been free from sad examples of them." (Mather: *Magnalia*, Bk. VI, Ch. VII.)

upon the breast: the ears were like an apes, and grew upon the shoulders; . . . it had on each foot three claws, with taleons like a fowl: upon the back above the belly it had a couple of great holes like mouths; and in each of them stood out a couple of pieces of flesh; it had no forehead, but above the eyes it had four horns; two of above an inch long, hard and sharp; and the other two somewhat less. The midwife was one strongly suspected of witchcraft; and a prime familist: thro' whose witchcrafts probably it came to pass, that most of the women present at the travel were suddenly taken with such a violent vomiting and purging, tho' they had neither eaten nor drunken any thing to occasion it, that they were forced immediately to go home; others had their children so taken with convulsions, which they never had before or after, that they also were sent for home immediately; whence none were left at the time of the monster's birth, but the midwife and two more, whereof one was fallen asleep: and about the time of the monster's death, which was two hours before his birth, such an odd shake was by invisible hands given to the bed as terrify'd the standers-by. It was buried without any noise of its monstrosity; but it being whispered a few days after about the town, the magistrates ordered the opening of the grave, whereby there was discovered this monstrum, horrendum, informe, ingens." [17]

Such works of the devil were regarded as commonplace, or, at least, as well attested facts of experience;

[17] Mather: *Magnalia*, Bk. VII, Ch. III, Sec. 11.

and when they became more numerous, as they naturally would, the holy zeal of the people of God became aroused. That the devil should be tolerated was, of course, ridiculous. The devil existed to be combated, and such combat with a supernatural power required a supreme effort. Of course, lacking knowledge of the causes, they could combat him only with zeal and not with intelligence. Nevertheless to their great relief, the troubles finally subsided, and they had the good grace to ascribe to God the credit and the glory. Thus the whole affair tended merely to strengthen their faith in the divine mission of New England.

These external struggles with the devil were as nothing compared with the internal conflicts of the churches. The very structure of the Holy Commonwealth itself proved to be one of its most serious difficulties. As long as there is unanimity, a Holy Commonwealth may be practical, but unanimity is precisely what is least apt to flourish in a new community, continually facing changing conditions, with no fixed body of precedent or law to dominate it. Even a secular state is precarious under such conditions, and a theocracy exaggerates these dangers. No one can live long in a Holy Commonwealth without becoming sensitive, irritable, losing his sense of values and ultimately his balance. All acts are acts either of God or of the devil; all issues are matters of religious faith; and all conflicts are holy wars. No matter how trivial an opinion might appear from a secular point of view, it became vital when promulgated as a theological dogma; no matter how harmless a fool might be, he was intolerable if he did not fit into the Covenant of Grace; no matter how slight an offense might be, it was a sin against Almighty God and hence infinite. Differences of opinion became differences of faith. Critics became blasphemers, and innovators, heretics. All the emotional fever which is normally pent up in religious experience was vented on any dispute which happened to arise. Issues which were trivial in their secular bearings became important and passionate because of the theological issues injected into them, and issues which would have been politically significant even in a secular society became much more so when loaded with holy passion and inflamed by religious fervor. In fact, the original pragmatic meaning of a question was not infrequently buried under layers of theological debate. Factions and sects hence multiplied even more rapidly than the population and spread like infectious fevers, so that within a few years New England was a hotbed of theological and political dispute, and within a few decades the Holy Commonwealth was literally exploded by the force of its own religious passion.

The appeal to the Bible merely made matters worse, for the Scriptures are sufficiently vague to stimulate rather than settle argument. No book not in need of interpretation can long remain a bible. Certainly the chief value of the Christian Bible for the Puritans was the fact that it could sanction anything at all. The appeal to its authority was synonymous with the attack on ecclesiastical authority and resulted in intellectual individualism or anarchy; for, in contrast to the definiteness of the dogmas of church and school, the Bible itself is no authority at all. It merely invites individual interpretation. The Bible, consequently, did not cramp the intellectual life of New England; it merely added the difficult technique of finding sanctions to the already difficult task of rational thinking, and it superimposed problems of scriptural criticism upon the already numerous problems of social life. Had there been conflicting authorities, the challenge would have been entirely to party struggles or even to arms; but when all parties appealed to the same authority, the challenge was to argument, or at least to verbal dispute. In short, the Bible stimulated free thinking, or at least free disputing, in New England. This was the very essence of Christian liberty, as the Protestants preached it, and the New England Puritans certainly abused this liberty to the utmost.

It is impossible here to recite the intricate story of these civil wars of the Lord; but it is necessary here to study several typical cases with a view to digging under the mass of theological debate, now largely unintelligible, to disclose the important issues, which, though buried beneath it, were really at its roots. There is, first of all, the case of that most conscientiously contentious of all the Puritans, whom Cotton Mather introduces as follows:

"In the year 1654, a certain Windmill in the Low

Countries, whirling round with extraordinary violence, by reason of a violent storm then blowing; the stone at length by its rapid motion became so intensely hot, as to fire the mill, from whence the flames, being dispersed by the high winds, did set a whole town on fire. But I can tell my reader, that about twenty years before this, there was a whole country in America like to be set on fire by the rapid motion of a windmill, in the head of one particular man. Know then, that about the year 1630, arrived here one Mr. Roger Williams." [18]

He, being a separatist, believed that the New England churches should have nothing to do with the Anglican Church and should definitely declare it to be no true church at all. Although there were many separatists in Massachusetts, notably at Plymouth and Salem, most Puritans were anxious to minimize the issue between them and the conformists as one of little importance, now that both parties were far enough removed from England to be able to cease quarreling about their relations to the Anglican Church. But Williams would not let the matter rest. He refused to join the Boston church because it would not definitely renounce all communion with the Anglican Church, publicly repent for ever having held such communion, and forbid its members when visiting in England to attend Anglican worship. He refused to attend informal meetings of the ministers around Boston, lest such meetings develop into a "presbytery or superintendency to the prejudice of the churches' liberties." He then not only began

[18] Mather: *Magnalia,* Bk. VII, Ch. II, Sec. 2.

to preach against the charter as a sinful instrument
of oppression, but also insisted that all the land be
purchased from the Indians, that the charter be publicly
forfeited, and that those colonists who for any reason
failed to compact with the natives should return to
England. He denied the right of the magistrates to
enforce the first table of the decalogue. He accused
King James of being a liar for saying that he was the
first Christian prince that had discovered this land, and
of being a blasphemer for calling Europe Christendom
or the Christian World. He persuaded Governor Endicott to cut the cross out of the flag on the ground that
it was an idolatrous and popish sign. He denounced
the resident's oath of allegiance, on the ground that it
was blasphemous to administer an oath to an unregenerate person. He went so far as to urge his people
not to pray with unregenerates, though they be members of their own families. Finally, when his own
church at Salem refused to renounce all communion
with its neighbor churches, he renounced it. He then
held meetings in his house at Plymouth. There are
always in any community a few amateur saints, usually
women, who are captivated by the earnest and persistent expositions of any idea, however foolish, in the
mouth of their own dear pastor, and who, once they see
the idea, will sacrifice everything else to it. Such a
pastor was Roger Williams, and such people now
gathered loyally around him in his home. Meantime
the court had decided to ship him back to England,
but, being advised privately by Governor Winthrop,

he fled to Narragansett Bay, where his small band joined him and founded Providence. Thus freed of all the New England churches, he began to seek a really genuine church, and, listening to some Anabaptists in the group, he was soon persuaded that his infant baptism was worthless and consented to be baptised by a farmer, named Ezekiel Hollyman, who had come from Salem. He soon discovered, however, that Mr. Hollyman's own baptism was worthless and that, therefore, he had no right to administer baptism to others. In fact, Williams became convinced that there was no one living with authority to baptise, and had not been since the days of the Apostles; that there was hence no such thing as a true church anywhere; and that he must wait for God to send a new apostle. In the meantime he organized his group into a fellowship of seekers, seeking that genuine church and final truth which had eluded him all his life! Accordingly in the charter for Rhode Island (for, although he had received his land from the Indians, he condescended to a royal charter) he gave equal privileges to all churches, since they were all alike mere human inventions. Rhode Island thus became a refuge for all sorts of religious misfits, or, as Cotton Mather put it, "It has been a colluvies of Antinomians, Familists, Anabaptists, Antisabbatarians, Arminians, Socinians, Quakers, Ranters, every thing in the world but Roman Catholicks, and real Christians, tho' of the latter, I hope there have been more than of the former among them; so that if a man had lost his religion, he might find it at the general muster of opinionists! The former generation of Rhode Islanders is now generally gone off the stage; . . . the rising generation, confounded by the contradictions in religion among their parents, are under many horrible temptations, and under some unhappy tendencies, to be of no religion at all." [19]

Thus it happened that the minister who, of all the New England clergy, was most violent in insisting that his own opinions prevail, became the father of religious toleration in this country. Roger Williams began by contending that he alone knew the truth, that all the New England churches should adopt his ideas, and that he would fight for them to the finish; he ended by denying all churches whatsoever, and seeking humbly both truth and peace, which, as he said, so rarely and seldom meet. He began by trying to make the Holy Commonwealth absolutely holy; he ended in a thorough disillusionment about the entire theory.

But that the Holy Commonwealth itself was at stake was not immediately apparent. Mr. Williams was at first regarded as a good Christian who merely had some queer notions, such as his obviously fantastic idea about the charter and the cross in the flag; they regarded him as one suffering "rather from a misguided conscience, than from a seditious principle." [20] But when he refused to recognize the magistrate's authority to enforce the first table of the decalogue, and when he virtually urged the Salem church to secede,

[19] Mather: *Magnalia*, Bk. VII, Ch. III, Sec. 12.
[20] *Ibid.*, Bk. VIII, Ch. II, Sec. 5.

he became a dangerous person. No doubt, if Salem church and Salem community had been more distinct, civil peace might not have been disturbed by his attacks on the churches; but, as we have seen, this distinction did not exist, and even had it existed in fact, it was vigorously denied in theory. Williams, himself, was at this time not certain where to draw the line between civil peace and church order. But during his persecution this distinction naturally was forced home on him, and when he finally succeeded in establishing a colony in which the distinction actually worked, in which religious anarchy was compatible with civil order, he not only discarded the philosophy of the Holy Commonwealth, but even made it the object of a vigorous attack. This culminated in the famous dispute between him and John Cotton, in which the issue was thoroughly debated. In 1644, Williams wrote *The Bloody Tenent of Persecution for cause of conscience discussed in a conference between Truth and Peace.* Cotton replied with *The Bloody Tenent washed white in the Blood of the Lambe.* To which Williams replied in 1652 with: *The Bloody Tenent yet more bloody by Mr. Cotton's endeavour to wash it white in the Blood of the Lambe; of whose precious Blood, spilt in the Blood of his Servants; and of the blood of millions spilt in former and later Wars for conscience sake, that most bloody Tenent of Persecution for cause of conscience, upon a second Tryal, is found more apparently and more notoriously guilty.* These writings consist of rational argument as well as appeals to the authority of Bible, princes, parliaments, and scholars, and they pertain not only to the particular questions of persecution but also to the whole philosophy of the relation between church and state, admonition and punishment, salvation and civil peace, soul and body. Cotton upheld consistently the philosophy of the Holy Commonwealth, claiming that fundamental heresies, of which any conscience can be convicted by admonition, are punishable by civil authorities, and likewise lesser errors when openly advocated in a seditious way. He quoted Moses freely. Williams, on the other hand, relied less on Moses and more on the authority of "that sweet spirit of Christian love." He pointed out that persecutors always have confused their opinions with the truth, that the civil power concerns merely the temporal welfare of man, and that tares and wheat should be allowed to grow together until God himself finally separates them. The argument on both sides is intricate and endless but the crux of the matter is evident: Cotton still had faith in the practicability of the Holy Commonwealth, whereas Williams took for granted that from a practical point of view the union of church and state actually implied persecution and civil strife, and that if truth and peace were ever to meet it were best to establish civil peace immediately on a secular basis and to let each seek the establishment of religious truth as best he could. Cotton and the Puritan ministers, in other words, revealed a deep-seated fear of religious dispute as a source of civil contention and moral anarchy; whereas Williams had a whole-hearted love of such dispute, seeing in it a sincere devotion to truth, and not alarming himself about its social consequences. We find Williams, for instance, as an old man of seventy, thoroughly enjoying a three-day debate with the Quakers. To him, it seems, Rhode Island was an ideal commonwealth precisely because it was continually engaged in sectarian dispute; to the leaders of Massachusetts it was for this very reason a most ungodly neighbor.

We turn now to an even more serious attack upon the Holy Commonwealth, growing out of the seemingly innocent endeavors of a pious woman, Anne Hutchinson. Like Roger Williams, this good woman was personally attractive and also an ardent worker in the church. She was especially serviceable to the women, not only in her capacity as a midwife, but also in her willingness to rehearse the pastor's sermons to those women who could not attend Sunday services. She was so skilful in expounding sermons that a number of women, and later a few men too, came to her house on Thursday evenings to hear her. At first she merely repeated the sermon, but gradually she ventured upon critical remarks, until finally, it seems, the prime interest in the meetings was Anne Hutchinson's estimate of Sunday's sermon. It soon appeared that she liked Mr. Cotton's sermons better than those of the other preachers in Boston. In fact she accused the other churches of being under the Covenant of Works, because they emphasized the moral character and Christian practice of their members, whereas she maintained that, in a genuine Covenant of Grace, all emphasis should be placed on the special work of God's redeeming grace by which a saint was made to feel sure of his election. In short, she complained that too much emphasis was put on the public morals of visible saints, and not enough on the invisible revelations of private experience; or, in the language of her time, no one has a right to accept even evident sanctification as evidence of his election without a concurrent sign of his justification.[21] When put in these words the issue appears to be sufficiently recondite to be allowed to pass as a theological luxury. But what was really at issue was the question of whether the churches should continue to be inclusive political organizations controlling the public life and morals of New England, or whether they were to become more exclusive bodies of the elect. The majority of the clergy were for the former policy, the policy which Anne Hutchinson called a Covenant of Works and which took for granted that sanctification and justification were in some way closely related; but the more extreme and fanatic group wanted the churches to be composed of those who were not merely sanctified (that is, leading sober, righteous and godly lives), but who were absolutely convinced of their justification or election by some special work of grace on their souls. Moreover they regarded all public works of the churches as evidence of the Covenant of Works, and used their formula to obstruct all govern-

---

21 She denied the possibility of "evidencing justification by sanctification." See C. F. Adams: *Antinomianism* (Boston, 1894), p. 123.

ment in worldly affairs. "The disturbance proceeded from thence into all the general affairs of the publick: the expedition against the Pequot-Indians was most shamefully discouraged, because the army was too much under a covenant of works; and the magistrates began to be contemned, as being of a legal spirit, and having therewithal a tang of Antichrist in them; nor could the ordering of town-lots, or town-rates, or any meetings whatsoever, escape the confusions of this controversie." [22]

Here again, if not the public peace itself, certainly the life of the Holy Commonwealth was really at stake. Had the churches taken the rigorous and logically consistent attitude of the Hutchinsonians, they would have lost most of their influence over public affairs; and "while saints were engaged in introspection, burly sinners would have run the commonwealth." Consequently most of the churches compromised by interpreting the Covenant of Grace in a moralistic and visible, rather than in an inner and pietistic, sense. "Those that are fit matter for a church, though they are not always able to make detailed relations of the work of grace, and the doctrine of Faith, yet must not live in the commission of any known sin, or the neglect of any known duty." [23] Or, to use the language of a later day, the early New England churches were committed to social rather than to evangelical Christianity. This position was evidently sensible from the point of view

[22] Mather: *Magnalia*, Bk. VII, Ch. III, Sec. 1.
[23] For this interpretation see Hooker's *Summe of Church Discipline*, and Stoddard's *Doctrine of Instituted Churches*, pp. 6 *ff*.

of public policy, but, as far as strict consistency goes, Anne Hutchinson no doubt had the better of the argument.

Another way in which she tended to undermine the Holy Commonwealth was by holding private meetings in her home. In fact, her followers were usually designated by her opponents as familists; and this familistical tendency was regarded as her most serious crime, for it undermined the public exercise and social dignity of religion, and in threatening church government it threatened all government. She admitted that she had no right to a public ministry, but she claimed something more divine, the gift of prophecy, and she frequently enforced her words with "the mouth of the Lord hath spoken it." The culminating blasphemy was her claim to be in bodily communion with the Holy Ghost. The clergy naturally were opposed to something so anti-clerical; but the issue was not merely between the vested clergy and the religious insurgents, it was between all those who conceived of religion as essentially a social and moral institution and those who regarded it as an inner experience of supernatural revelation. The purport and tendency of the familist movement was admittedly antinomian or anarchistic; Anne Hutchinson thus provided the official sanction and philosophy for all sorts of malcontents.

In the case both of Roger Williams and of Anne Hutchinson, it is altogether too easy for us to appraise them from the point of view of later issues, rather than of their contemporary significance. They did not represent primarily the struggle between theocratic autocracy and religious toleration.[24] Looking back, it is obvious to us that, from the point of view of later developments, this aspect of the case is most significant; but from the point of view of the problems of the founding of New England, they represent rather a struggle between fanatical religion and moral religion, between socially irresponsible and socially effective churches, between visible and invisible Christianity. The clergy, to be sure, were on the side of the magistrates, and the magistrates were on the side of law and order; but the practical alternative to law and order at this time was not liberty but fanaticism. It is dangerous to generalize about this situation, but if we must generalize, it is reasonably accurate to say that most of the clergy and most of the people usually compromised their theological theories in view of practical exigencies, and that the clergy were on the whole even more ready to keep an eye on the demands of ordinary political good sense than the laity, since the laity, being less directly responsible for the corporate life of the colonies, were more apt to yield to theological dialectics and to erratic fanatics regardless of consequences. Whether this be true or not in general, it is clearly so of the two cases here before us. To us, no doubt, the rulers of the Holy Commonwealth seem fanatic; but in view of such characters as Roger Williams and

<hr>

[24] *Cf.* the accounts of Brooks Adams: *The Emancipation of Massachusetts* (Boston and New York, 1887); J. T. Adams: *The Founding of New England* (Boston, 1921); Winifred K. Rugg: *Unafraid* (Boston, 1930); and others.

Anne Hutchinson, they exhibited a relatively large amount of sober judgment.

The case of the familists would not have been quite so significant had it not incidentally forced the consideration of even more fundamental problems. In its social setting, the issue raised by Anne Hutchinson was fairly simple, but in its theological dialectics, it was so intricate that even the clergy became hopelessly confused, and when they were forced to compare notes they discovered, to their dismay, that there was such a variety of opinions on these points that it was impossible to tell which were truth and which error. Consequently, in spite of their political prejudices against synods and anything that smacked of centralized church government, they were forced in 1637 to call a ministerial convention, soon frankly called a synod, in order to find out who was in error. No less than eighty-two debatable points were brought up. It soon appeared that those who expounded the will of God needed to come to some sort of mutual agreement and understanding if they did not want to appear ridiculous in their pretensions. Accordingly, after discovering how the predominant opinion stood, they set up each error, not however for the sake of enforcing it, but merely for the sake of declaring it. "The error being first fairly recited, there was only a short reflection made upon it after this manner—this is contrary to such and such a text of scripture, (then and there subjoined) which in the quotation thereof being briefly applied unto the case, did unto reasonable men immediately smite the error under the fifth rib." [25] Mr. Cotton's case proved the most difficult, for though he desired to be orthodox, he found himself able to hold his own in argument against the great majority of his brethren. "There were five questions offered unto that great man, unto which questions he gave answers; and unto those answers the synod gave replies; and unto those replies he gave returns; and unto those returns the synod gave rejoinders; till their collisions fetch'd I know not whether more light or love unto one another." [26]

This proved to be merely the beginning. Another convention was necessary in 1643. In 1645, Hooker was asked to write an authoritative *Summe of Church-Discipline*. This merely led to the Cambridge Synod of 1646-8, with its famous Platform. Then came the Assembly of 1657, and the Synod of 1662, which decided on the Half-Way Covenant. Again in 1667, 1679,

[25] Mather: *Magnalia,* Bk. VII, Ch. III, Sec. 4.
[26] Mather: *Magnalia,* Bk. VII, Ch. III, Sec. 5, continues: "Because 'twill not be easie to give a fair and full representation of what passed on paper, I shall not now trouble the world with the debated questions, much less with the debates upon the questions: . . . But after sorrowful discourses pro and con, upon these arguments, Mr. Cotton the next morning made an excellent speech unto the assembly, tending towards an accommodation of the controversie. . . . The synod greedily and joyfully laid hold on the reconciling offers of Mr. Cotton; and they at length agreed, that we are not united and married unto the Lord Jesus Christ without faith, giving an actual consent of soul unto it; That God's effectual calling of the soul unto the Lord Jesus Christ, and the soul's apprehending by an act of faith the offered righteousness of the Lord Jesus Christ is in order of nature before God's act of justification upon the soul: That in the testimony of the holy Spirit, which is the evidence of our good estate before God, the qualifications of inherent graces, and the fruits thereof, proving the sincerity of our faith must ever be co-existent, concurrent, co-apparent, or else the conceived testimony of the Spirit is either a delusion or doubtful. An happy conclusion of the whole matter."

1680, and so on. In short, the synod became a frequent and necessary institution. All this is evidence that control was becoming increasingly difficult. Each synod was a symptom of differences, and each left its disaffected minority. Authority became more centralized, government more autocratic, and Hooker's vision of the democracy of the little Kingdoms of Christ, wherein they shall teach no more every man his neighbor, faded into a dream. The theocracy became a government by the influential clergy and the Holy Commonwealth degenerated into an ecclesiastical autocracy.

Added to these internal disruptive tendencies, or civil wars of the Lord, there were a number of external agencies undermining the church order of New England. In the first place, other sects and churches were making invasions. Quakers, Anglicans, Anabaptists, and later, Methodists, were forming congregations and carrying on propaganda. These churches were content to be merely churches; to them the idea of the Holy Commonwealth was meaningless. All they asked of the civil order was peace and security. And all the Holy Commonwealth in turn asked of them was non-interference. The general policy of the Puritans toward these outsiders seems to have been to ignore them as long as they did not make trouble for the commonwealth, but as soon as they caused any disturbance, they were persecuted, or, to give the Puritans the benefit of the doubt, prosecuted, without stint or scruple. The Reverend Nathaniel Ward, of Ipswich, to be sure, took it upon himself "to bee the Herauld of New-England so farre, as to proclaime to the world, in the name of our Colony, that all Familists, Antinomians, Anabaptists and other Enthusiasts shall have free Liberty to keepe away from us, and such as will come to be gone as fast as they can, the sooner the better. I dare, averre, that God doth no where in his word tolerate Christian States, to give Tolerations to such adversaries of his Truth, if they have power in their hands to suppresse them. . . . Not to tolerate things meerly indifferent to weak consciences, argues a conscience too strong: pressed uniformity in these, causes much disunity: To tolerate more than indifferents, is not to deale indifferently with God. . . . He that is willing to tolerate any Religion, or discrepant way of Religion, besides his own, unlesse it be in matters meerly indifferent, either doubts of his own, or is not sincere in it. That State that will give Liberty of Conscience in matters of Religion, must give Liberty of Conscience and Conversation in their Morall Laws, or else the Fiddle will be out of tune, and some of the strings crack." [27]

This represents the philosophy, rather than the facts. As long as other sects behaved indifferently they were treated as matters merely indifferent. This negative sort of toleration, this ignoring of irrelevant sects, was freely indulged in, and as time went on there was a large number of settlers of other denominations who

---

[27] Nathaniel Ward: *The Simple Cobler of Aggavvam in America* (London, 1647). In Hart: *American History Told by Contemporaries*, pp. 393-5.

even erected their own churches without being molested, except in that they had no rights of citizenship.
But these aliens inevitably caused trouble. The peace-
loving Quakers seem to have been the most militant dis-
turbers of the Puritan peace. Individual Quakers, not
able to hold their own meetings, made a practice of
attending whatever public worship happened to be
established. But unfortunately it was part of their religion not merely to attend but also to participate in
the meetings. Accordingly it frequently happened that
after the sermon a Quaker would arise to make his own
testimony. Even this infringement of the order of public worship seems to have been tolerated in many instances, but when these post-sermon remarks of Quakers began to assume the character of criticism, the
magistrates immediately interfered, not in the name of
protecting the clergy, but in defense of public order.
Both parties were, of course, intolerant, but an inter-
ference with public worship would even today be regarded as a civil offense. This use of force by civil
authority was precisely the most fundamental of
Quaker aversions, and, when they were thus proceeded
against, they heroically became martyrs. Matters
quickly grew worse. Repeated offenses called for
severer punishments. Severer punishments called for
sterner rebukes. Finally, when it was discovered, under these strained circumstances, that Quakers would
not remove their hats in court nor address the judge
with "your honor," they were regarded as the most extreme antinomians, which they were, and banished as

anarchists who were trying to undermine not only God's churches but civil authority in general. Several Quakers, after repeated offenses, were ordered banished on pain of death, but they were naturally moved by the Spirit to testify to the truth, piously undergoing martyrdom rather than cowardly running away from their persecutors. This put the Puritan authorities in a bad predicament. They tried all the varieties of force—imprisonment, cutting off ears and tongues, whipping and other tortures—hoping by these means to stave off the unpopular spectacle of executing people who, in the face of death, behaved like real followers of Christ. But naturally the more they tried force, the more force they had to try. Finally they hanged two men and having placed Mary Dyer's head in the noose to frighten her sufficiently, they forcibly banished her, thus avoiding the very distasteful task of making a woman martyr. But after a few months in Rhode Island, Mary's conscience triumphed; she returned to Massachusetts and was hanged. These few martyrs, it seems, were sufficient to temper the holy enthusiasm of both parties. The Puritans, hereafter, were with difficulty provoked into arresting Quakers, and the Quakers became less inclined to give offense. Many quietly held their own meetings and many more moved quietly to neighboring lands which were just as cheap and both more fertile and more free.

In the case of the Quakers, even more than in those of Roger Williams and Anne Hutchinson, the fundamental causes of the disturbances were no doubt public

and civil conflicts rather than theological differences.
But when it came to argument, and even to court trials,
the emphasis was placed on the heretical ideas which
were supposed to underlie these anarchistic practices.
The Quaker emphasis on the inner light was interpreted to be an attack on the validity of the revelations
in Holy Scriptures; the Quaker identification of the
voice of conscience with the spirit of Christ was regarded as sheer blasphemy. But anyone who takes the
trouble to examine these theological controversies can
easily see that the moral and political issues were fundamental to the theological, and not *vice versa*. The
mere fact that the disputes with the Quakers became
so violent and were conducted with so much mutual
hatred is circumstantial evidence that there were underlying social differences. In the popular mind, as a matter of fact, almost any disorder arising from the lower
classes was identified with Quakerism. Beggars,
thieves, roving lunatics, were held up as typical Quakers, and the violent repudiations of such persons on
the part of the Quakers merely promoted the popular
superstition. Cotton Mather's description of the Quakers [28] is, of course, partisan, false, and libellous, but it
is good evidence of the fact that the Quaker controversy
centered about social, rather than intellectual, issues.
Mather, in his day, and also earlier generations of cler-
ical aristocrats, looked upon the Quakers as morally
and socially the scum of the earth. Their militant paci-
fism and democracy, combined with their usual poverty

[28] See his *Magnalia*, Bk. VIII, Ch. IV.

and illiteracy, made them disgusting to the proud and prosperous Yankees. Hence on both sides the conflict soon issued in campaigns of mutual vituperation, rather than in a critical discussion of the basic moral and intellectual issues which separated them. The following passage from Cotton Mather is probably sufficient evidence not only of the *ad hominem* nature of the argument on both sides, but also of the fact that the wars of the Lord with the Quakers in Massachusetts belong to the history of class struggles, rather than of ideas:

"I can foretel what usage I shall find among the Quakers: . . . for a worthy man that writes of them has observed, for pride, and hypocrisie, and hellish reviling against the painful ministers of Christ, I know no people can match them. Yea, prepare, friend Mather, to be assaulted with such language as Fisher the Quaker, in his pamphlets, does bestow upon such men as Dr. Owen; thou fiery fighter and green-headed trumpeter; thou hedghog and grinning dog; thou bastard that tumbled out of the mouth of the Babilonish bawd; thou mole; thou tinker; thou lizzard; thou bell of no metal, but the tone of a kettle; thou wheelbarrow; thou whirlpool; thou whirlegig. O thou firebrand; thou adder and scorpion; thou louse; thou cow-dung; thou moon-calf; thou ragged tatterdemallion; thou Judas; thou livest in philosophy, and logick which are of the devil. . . . These are the very words, (I wrong them not!) which they vomit out against the best men in the English nation, that have been so hardy as to touch their light within; but let the quills of these porcupines fly as fast as they will, I shall not feel them! Yea, every stone that these Kildebrands throw at me, I will wear as a pearl; and as Dr. Holland, when he took his leave of his friends, would say, I will here take my leave, with saying, I commend thee to the love of God, and the dislike of Quakerism." [29]

These wars with the Quakers, though not fertile in the clarification of intellectual issues, are none the less very significant in the history of the idea of the Holy Commonwealth, for they were the earliest of the major conflicts to reveal the fact that the Holy Commonwealth was losing its popular sympathies and catholic basis. The self-styled best men of New England were the champions of the political cause of the Lord, whereas the common people were forcing the clergy and the courts, in deference to public sentiment, to compromise the purity of New England. Thus the churches gradually discovered that the external wars of the Lord were in the end less disastrous than the internal decay of the saints, which transformed them from the elect of the Kingdom of God into the élite of New England. They were forced to choose between remaining loyal to the Holy Commonwealth, in the hope that it would soon be established in heaven instead of in Boston, and remaining loyal to New England, though it refused to be holy. In the end, as we shall see, they took the latter alternative.

[29] Mather: *Magnalia,* Bk. VII, Ch. IV, Sec. 3.

CHAPTER III

THE LOSS OF THE SENSE OF SIN

The Holy Commonwealth was, from the start, an idea, not a fact. Even among the passengers on the *Mayflower,* only thirty-five out of the one hundred and two were of the Leyden congregation, the remaining sixty-seven being a very "mixed lot from London." "Some of the London element boasted openly that they did not intend to be ruled by anyone, but would use their own liberty." [1] Lechford wrote in 1640: "Here is required such confessions, and professions, both in private and publique, both by men and women, before they be admitted, that three parts of the people of the Country remaine out of the Church, so that in short time most of the people will remaine unbaptized." [2] Mr. Cotton vigorously denied this, claiming that "it is not true, that three parts of the Countrey remaine out of the Church, if he meane three parts of foure, no, though hee should take in those remote English, who live a score of miles or more from any Church." [3] But Cotton gives no estimate of his own.

[1] See James Truslow Adams: *The Founding of New England* (Boston, 1921), p. 98.
[2] Thomas Lechford: *Plain Dealing, or News from New England* (London, 1642), pp. 150-1.
[3] John Cotton: *Way of Congregational Churches Cleared* (London, 1648), Pt. I, p. 72.

In 1635, a law was passed in Massachusetts making church attendance compulsory, and in 1638, every resident was taxed for the ministry, whether church member or not. At the same time it was enacted that an excommunicated person must endeavor to have himself restored within six months! In 1631, Massachusetts Bay passed a law requiring church membership of all freemen or enfranchised citizens. Up to 1643, out of a probable population of over 15,000 in Massachusetts, 1708 had been admitted as freemen. In Plymouth, where no church membership test was required, the proportion was even smaller: out of about 3000 inhabitants in 1643, only 230 were enfranchised. In 1674, the number of freemen in Massachusetts was 2527.[4]

It is easy to misinterpret these facts. In the first place, a distinction must be made between church members and church attendants. Though comparatively few belonged to the elect and were hence in full communion, the great majority even of the unregenerate attended church. It was not until 1635 that it was thought necessary to have a law requiring church attendance. The distinction between the church and the congregation was familiar and endured well into the eighteenth century, when membership in the church was easier than it had been in the seventeenth century. We have every reason to believe that, until about 1640,

---

[4] For these statistics and their interpretation see J. T. Adams: *The Founding of New England,* pp. 97, 98, 121, 132, 142, 144, 172; Herbert L. Osgood: *The American Colonies in the Seventeenth Century,* Vol. I, pp. 211-3; George E. Ellis: *The Puritan Age and Rule in the Colony of Massachusetts Bay 1629-1685,* Ch. VI; Williston Walker: *The Creeds and Platforms of Congregationalism,* pp. 165-7.

at least, the majority of the population were in general sympathy with the churches and their Holy Commonwealth, whether they were church members or not. In fact, until 1638, there was a definite economic motive for not joining a church, because only church members were asked to support the churches. After that date, when all residents were taxed alike, there naturally arose a demand for a more easy method of admission to membership.

The citizenship statistics are also easily misleading. It has frequently been assumed that, since *only* church members could be freemen, therefore *all* male church members were freemen, on the general supposition that the franchise was a privilege which no qualified church member would neglect. But it by no means follows that, because only one out of five men, to take the traditional estimate, were freemen, therefore church membership was equally small. The background of the New England settlers was not democratic. They were accustomed to a very limited suffrage even in England. Besides, we must remember that these settlements were primarily trading adventures, financed by stock companies, and that initially only members of the company were entitled to the rights of freemen. Thus, at first, over ninety-nine per cent of the population was disenfranchised and it was taken for granted that the office of exercising political rights belonged to a very small class. Citizenship was looked upon as a burden and in one instance, at least, the attempt was made to force church members by law to make application for the privileges of freemen. Especially the outlying settlers expected no rights and assumed no responsibilities. Frontiersmen are always individualists. There is every reason to believe, therefore, that the number of those qualified to become freemen was considerably larger than those who actually availed themselves of the opportunity. As time went on, of course, and party differences appeared, the demand for the franchise gradually grew, but even well into the eighteenth century, it was by no means generally believed that all who were taxed had a right to be represented by men of their own choosing.

In short, it is difficult to estimate accurately the varying strength of the churches in New England; nevertheless historians now agree on the general outlines of the story. The philosophy of the Holy Commonwealth, though it expressed the aims of the churches, was never a true picture of New England society. Church members were a decided minority from the first and even those who were in sympathy with the theocracy were, after 1650 and possibly even before that, an increasingly small minority. The philosophy of the Holy Commonwealth, far from being a statement of fact, soon became merely the ideal of only a minority. The original elect, surrounded by a howling wilderness and seeking comfort in their distress, soon became the social elect, surrounded by the unregenerates over whom they attempted to tyrannize. The theory of God's sovereignty ceased to be the spontaneous product of a pious imagination and became the instrument of oppression in the hands of an ecclesiastical oligarchy.

This philosophy not only misrepresented the facts of New England society, but also over-simplified the intellectual life of New England. It served well enough as an official halo, or rationalization, in the absence of a better one, but it did not represent the actual aims and motives of all the settlers. Cotton Mather tells the story of how a minister from the Bay went to some plantations to the northward of New Plymouth and "urged them to approve themselves a religious people from this consideration, that otherwise they would contradict the main end of planting this wilderness; whereupon a well-known person, then in the assembly, cryed out, Sir, you are mistaken, you think you are preaching to the people at the Bay; *our* main end was to catch fish." [5] That there were many, even in the Bay, whose main end was to catch fish is also beyond doubt.

The truth is that the motives which actually operated in New England were many and mixed. Even Thomas Shepard, one of the most pious of the Puritan preachers, when he came.to set down his reasons for emigrating gives us this interesting catalogue: "The reasons which swayed me to come to New England were many. 1. I saw no call to any other place in Old England nor way of subsistence in peace and comfort to me and my family. 2. Diverse people in Old England of my dear friends desired me to goe

[5] Mather: *Magnalia,* Pt. I, Bk. I, Ch. IV, Sec. 2.

to N. E. there to live together, . . . 3. I saw the Lord departed from England when Mr. Hooker and Mr. Cotton were gone, and I saw the harts of most of the godly set and bent that way, and I did think I should feele many miseries if I stayed behind. 4. My judgement was then convinced not only of the evil of ceremonies, but of mixt communion. . . . 5. I saw it my duty to desire the fruition of all God's ordinances, which I could not enjoy in Old England. 6. My dear wife did much long to see me settled there in peace and so put me on to it. 7. Although it was true I should stay and suffer for Christianity, yet I saw no rule for it now the Lord had opened a doore of escape; otherwise I did incline much to stay and suffer especially after our sea stormes. 8. Tho' my ends were mixt and I looked much to my own quiet, yet the Lord let me see the glory of those liberties in N. England." [6] Which of all these was the real reason, God only knows— Marx and Freud notwithstanding. Suffice it to say here that the Puritans were internally and externally a mixture of many elements.

This original intellectual complexity of the situation was exaggerated by political and economic factors. The Puritans of their own strength might have kept New England holy, but in order to keep it at all, and to give it the necessary economic footing, they were compelled to invite outsiders by adopting a very liberal land policy. In freely granting large tracts of land to individual settlers, New England encouraged a rapid

[6] Thomas Shepard: *Autobiography* (Boston, 1832), pp. 42-3.

immigration not only from Old England but even from the West Indies and other American colonies as well. These people made New England prosper, but they helped undermine its moral and intellectual solidarity.

While these forces were undermining the theocracy at home, other enemies were gathering abroad. Gorges, whose land grants conflicted with those of the Puritans, had associated with him several disaffected persons, who, like Thomas Morton, "our host of Merry-mount," had been driven out of Massachusetts by the holy zeal of the magistrates. These men were clamoring at the King's Court against the colony, using Puritan intolerance, and any other available accusation, as pretexts for urging a revocation of the charter. Knowing this, the Puritans were forced to relax their holy endeavors a bit, in order not to feed more fuel to these *émigrés*. Most serious of all was the precariousness of the Holy Commonwealth after the restoration of the Stuarts and the re-assertion of their claims to divine sovereignty.

If we may doubt the first generation's preoccupation with the Kingdom of God, we may become increasingly sceptical of the second and third generations. The first generation worked continually and concertedly. Some worked in forest and field; others at building ships; still others traded in fish, furs, lumber and rum. Some worked to maintain political order in the face of chaos; others labored for the Kingdom of

God. All worked. Not even Puritans worked merely for the love of it; they worked of necessity. They rested from their daily labors every seventh day, but even Sunday was devoted to serious intellectual work. They could not afford to celebrate the many traditional holidays and feast days of Old England. The celebration of Christmas Day itself was looked upon as "popery." There is a famous incident, told in Bradford's *History of Plymouth,* concerning a company of new arrivals in the colony.

"On the day called Christmas Day the Governor called them out to work, (as was used) but the most of this new-company excused themselves, and said it went against their consciences to work on that day. So the Governor told them that if they made it matter of conscience, he would spare them, till they were better informed; so he led away the rest and left them; but when they came home at noone, from their work, he found them in the street at play openly; some pitching the bar, and some at stoole-ball, and such like sports. So he went to them, and took away their implements, and told them, that was against his conscience, that they should play, and others worke; if they made the keeping it matter of devotion, let them keep their houses, but there should be no gaming, or revelling in the streets. Since which time nothing hath been attempted that way, at least openly." [7]

In 1628 Thomas Morton and his company, having

[7] William Bradford: *History of the Plymouth Plantation.* In Hart, p.

established themselves on Merry-mount, "prepared to sett up a Maypole upon the festival day of Philip and Jacob; and therefore brewed a barrel of excellent beer, and provided a case of bottles to be spent; with other good cheare, for all commers of that day. And because they would have it in a compleat forme, they had prepared a song fitting to the time and present occasion. And upon Mayday they brought the Maypole to the place appointed, with drumes, gunnes, pistols, and other fitting instruments, for that purpose. . . . This harmless mirth made by young men (that lived in hope to have wifes brought over to them, that would save them a laboure to make a voyage to fetch any over) was much distasted, of the precise Separatists: that keepe much a doe about the tythe of mint and cummin; troubling their braines more then reason would require about things that are indifferent: and from that time sought occasion against my honest Host of Ma-re Mount to overthrow his ondertakings, and to destroy his plantation quite and cleane." [8] Even such innocent and "indifferent" celebrations were forbidden, theoretically, of course, because they were unscriptural, but really because they were economically dangerous. The Puritans were physically compelled to concentrate on their task. Their character was as severe as their domestic furnishings, and for the same reason.

This Puritan thrift soon produced Yankee prosperity, and Yankee prosperity produced urban aristocracies. The precariousness of the frontier gave place to the

[8] Thomas Morton: *New English Canaan.* In Hart, pp. 362-3.

security of the towns. Luxury gradually crept in. The younger generations could afford to rest a bit on their fathers' oars. They had not undergone the moral discipline of the frontier. They did not realize what it cost to found New England. To them New England was home, not a howling wilderness. Consequently their fathers' strenuous standards began to irritate them, and the philosophy of God's wonder-working providence began to take on a hollow sound. But if the children complained of the severity of their fathers, the fathers complained of the worldliness of their children. No one willingly sees his offspring consume what he has laboriously produced, even though he may have produced it for that very purpose. The early standards were accordingly preached to the youth and upheld as inherently worthy of obedience; their original practical value being less conspicuous, they were enforced by religious sanctions. Prohibitions were made and restraining laws enacted. Waste of time became inherently bad and diversions became sins by divine commandment.

Cotton Mather, for example, declared: "The general rules, which in all recreations are to be observed, are so generally transgressed in these games [of cards or dice] that ordinarilly it can be no other than a sin to use them. These diversions fascinate the minds of those that practice them, at such a rate, that if ever those persons come to be converted unto God, they bitterly lament the loss of time in which that practice hath involved them. And the many other passions and follies almost inseparable from these diversions, render the diversions themselves to be sins against the commandments, which prohibit the evils thereby occasioned." [9]

In 1653, the General Court at Boston was aroused to action. "Upon information of sundry abuses and misdemeanors committed by several persons on the Lord's Day, not only by children playing in the streetes and other places, but by youthes, maydes, and other persons, both straungers and others, uncivilly walkinge the streetes and feilds, travilling from towne to towne, goeing on ship-board, frequentinge common houses and other places to drinke, sport, and otherwise to mispend that precious time, which thinges tend much to the dishonor of God, the reproach of religion, and the prophanation of his holy Sabbath, the sanctification whereof is sometime put for all dutyes immediately respectinge the service of God conteined in the first table; it is therefore ordered by this Court and the authoritie, that no children, youths, maydes, or other persons shall transgress in the like kind on penalty of beinge reputed great provokers of the high displeasure of Almighty God, and further incurringe the penaltyes hereafter expressed." [10]

Even the ministers, though they railed against worldliness, were infected with pride in their worldly prosperity. Note, for example, the exultant worldliness ill-concealed in this defense of religion: "When the Lord

[9] Mather: *Magnalia*, Bk. V, Pt. 2, Ch. XVII.
[10] See George E. Ellis: *The Puritan Age and Rule in the Colony of Massachusetts Bay* (Boston and New York, 1888), pp. 225-6.

84

stirred up the spirits of so many of his people to come over into this wilderness, it was not for Worldly Wealth, or a better livelihood for the outward man. The generality of the people that came over, professed the contrary: Nor had we any rational grounds to expect such a thing in such a wilderness. Tho' God hath blessed his poor people here, and there are that have increased here, from small beginnings to great estates; That the Lord may call this whole generation to witness.—O Generation see! Look upon your towns and fields, Look upon your habitations and shops, and ships, and behold your numerous posterity, and great increase in the blessings of the Land and Sea; Have I been a wilderness unto you? We must needs answer, No, Lord, Thou hast been a gracious God, and exceeding good unto thy servants, even in these earthly blessings; we live in a more plentiful and comfortable manner than ever we did expect." [11]

The older clergy were thus placed more and more on the defensive. They bewailed the degenerate times. "As to New England's First Ways: What glorious things might be spoken to the praise of free grace. But O! what a sad metamorphosis hath there of later years past upon these churches and plantations?—It must be spoken in the name of the Lord, O New England, Thy God expects better things from thee and thy children; not worldliness;—not an itching after new things and ways;—not a drawing loose in the yoke of God? Alas!

[11] *The Cause of God, and his People in New England; stated in a sermon of the memorable Mr. John Higginson, unto the General Court of Massachusetts Colony, May 27, 1663* (Cambridge), pp. 10-11.

How is New-England, in danger of being lost even in New-England?" [12]

In the Cambridge Platform of 1648, it had been agreed that children of members of the Church Covenant of Grace were also members.[13] However, these members by birth, when they came of age, were expected to make public profession of personal regeneration before they were admitted to the Holy Communion. When the time came, many of this second generation did not make such a personal profession; nevertheless they not only regarded themselves as full members, but asked to have their children baptised. This brought the issue to a head. Had the churches yielded to this demand, the great majority of the third generation of church members, no doubt, would have been unregenerate. Had the church not yielded at all, and insisted that even the second generation should be excluded from the church unless they professed regeneration, the churches would have lost many of their younger and most influential members. In either case the Holy Commonwealth was doomed. In this dilemma, which was debated in the Ministerial Convention of 1657 and the Synod of 1662, the decision to compromise was finally reached. The unregenerate second generation were allowed to remain in church and to have their children baptised into the church;

[12] *New England's True Interest further declared, in the words of the Hon. William Stoughton, Esq., in a sermon preached by him . . . April, 1668* (Boston, 1774), pp. 19-20.

[13] Ch. 3, Par. 2; and Ch. 12, Par. 7. See also the discussion above, in Ch. I.

but neither they nor their children were allowed to become partakers of the Lord's Supper—they were said to be members, but not in full communion. This was the famous Half-Way Covenant which the churches were compelled to adopt in practice, though several generations of theologians, as we shall see, struggled in vain to justify it in theory.[14]

The chief stumbling-block in the whole question was the practice of exacting public relations of the regenerating work of grace, before a person could claim divine election and membership in the Covenant of Grace. Rather than undergo this ordeal, which was usually both embarrassing and stultifying, sinners were content to remain in their natural state and forego the privileges of communion. Thus, within a comparatively short time, the churches were composed, for the most part, of technically unregenerate persons, known as baptised adult non-communicants. All parties usually accepted this state of affairs in good humor, as a sensible evasion of an issue which, if insisted upon, would only have made everybody uncomfortable.

The first serious threat to the Half-Way Covenant came in 1698, when a group of wealthy and influential trustees of Harvard College, who had incurred the hostility of President Increase Mather, revolted and organized an independent church in Brattle Street, Boston. In this group was Thomas Brattle, whose father was one of the wealthiest men in New England,

---

[14] See Ch. VII. For the text of the Half-Way Covenant see Williston Walker: *The Creeds and Platforms of Congregationalism* (New York, 1893).

and who, himself, was a prosperous business-man. He had spent several years in England after his graduation from Harvard and was strongly inclined toward the Anglican type of worship. He was an astronomer and mathematician. In 1692, he had opposed the witch-craft scare in which Increase Mather was involved. His brother, William Brattle, was minister at Cambridge and a tutor at Harvard. In his church the public relation of experiences was discontinued about the year 1696; and, though he raised no theological issues in his sermons which his fellow-ministers could dispute, he emphasized increasingly the practical moral problems of the day and the idea of God's great mercy. These two brothers, together with John Leverett (later President of Harvard), gathered around them some very respectable and prosperous citizens of Boston, as well as several other members of Harvard College; they built a church in Brattle Square and invited Benjamin Colman to be their minister. Colman was a Harvard graduate who had been preaching in non-conformist churches in England since 1695. On the advice of the Brattle Street group, he arranged to be ordained by the Presbytery in London before returning to Boston. He arrived, therefore, fully ordained and completely independent of the Boston Association controlled by Increase Mather, and the church was thus a direct challenge to the New England theocracy. The "undertakers of the New Church" immediately issued a Manifesto which contained, among others, the following principles: (1) Loyalty was pledged to the Westminster Confession.

(2) Selections from the Scriptures were to be read without comment by the minister. (3) Baptism was to be administered, not only to "such as professed faith and obedience to Christ and to their children," but also to the children of "any professed Christians" who engaged to educate the children in the Christian religion. (4) Communion might be received only by "persons of visible sanctity," and the pastor was responsible for ascertaining such sanctity. (5) "But we assume not to ourselves to impose upon any a public relation of their experiences." (6) If any fell into "scandalous sin" they might be excommunicated by the pastor with the consent of the brethren. (7) "A particular church is a society of Christians by mutual agreement." (8) All baptised persons, women, as well as men, who contributed to the maintenance of the church, were to have a vote in electing the minister.

This Manifesto caused a sensation among the ministers. Increase Mather attempted to force the authors to retract it, and, when he failed, he wrote a vigorous pamphlet, *The Order of the Gospel, Professed and Practiced by the Churches of Christ in New England, Justified.* The ministers of Salem wrote a long letter of advice in which they urged the Brattle Street men to read a famous pamphlet, *Spiritual Milk for Boston Babes drawn out of the Breasts of both Testaments;* they condemned them for the self-confident and arrogant way in which they had disregarded the other churches and their disciplines; they accused them of laxity in the matters of communion, public relations,

and baptism; and they concluded by stating that "the females are certainly more than the males and consequently the choice of ministers is put into their hands. . . . It is certain the baptized adult non-communicants in most if not all the assemblies in the land, are more than the communicants, and consequently, if they should take their rule and manners from this article [of the Manifesto], they might make worse work in all the churches than we are willing to say." [15] And someone contributed "a simple poem upon the authors and their design" which concluded:
"Our churches turn genteel:
"Our parsons grow trim and trig,
"With wealth, wine and wig
"And their heads are covered with meal." [16]
These documents reveal quite clearly what was happening, not only in Brattle Street, but also throughout New England. The genteel churches were turning from the gospel of election and regeneration; they were content to be simply "societies of Christians by mutual agreement"; and to be Christians meant merely to "profess faith in and obedience to Christ" and to avoid "scandalous sin." In other words, these respectable Yankees wished thenceforth to be known as Christians, not as unregenerates. Yet all this growing pride could be accompanied by lip-service to the Westminster Confession and the doctrine of depravity. The theory

[15] Samuel K. Lothrop: *A History of the Church in Brattle Street, Boston* (Boston, 1851), p. 34.
[16] *Ibid.*, p. 40. For the literature of this controversy see the bibliography for this chapter.

remained intact, though the sinners disappeared.

The Brattle Street church issue, however, still left the question of communion in the old embarrassing form. The responsibility for determining visible sanctity was shifted from the participant himself to the minister, but theoretically the sacrament of communion could not be administered so liberally as that of baptism. And in general the ministers believed that their "main duty was to communicants." [17]   To meet this situation, the Reverend Solomon Stoddard, of Northampton, revised the theory of the communion. In his *Doctrine of Instituted Churches* (1700), the theory was developed that the Lord's Supper was not primarily a sacred privilege of the elect, but a means of salvation, and should therefore be administered to the unregenerate provided they were of good conversation. He answered boldly to the question: "Whether such persons as have a good conversation and a competent knowledge, may come to the Lords Supper, with a good conscience, in case they know themselves to be in a natural condition? Answ. They may and ought to come tho they know themselves to be in a natural condition; this ordinance is instituted for all the adult members of the Church who are not scandalous, and therefore must be attended by them; as no man may neglect prayer, or hearing the Word, because he cannot do it in faith, so he may not neglect the Lords Supper." [18]

[17] Increase Mather, cited in K. B. Murdock: *Increase Mather: The Foremost American Puritan* (Cambridge, 1925), p. 363.
[18] Solomon Stoddard: *The Doctrine of Instituted Churches, explained and proved from the Word of God* (London, 1700), p. 21.

Increase Mather came to the rescue of the traditional theory in his *Order of the Gospel;* and in reply to it, Stoddard further developed his theory by saying: "This Ordinance has a proper tendency in its own to convert men. Herein men may learn the necessity and sufficiency of the death of Christ in order to Pardon. Here is an affecting offer of Christ crucifyed; here is a sealing of the Covenant, that if men come to Christ, they shall be saved, which is a great means to convince of safety in coming to Christ. All Ordinances are for the saving good of those that they are to be administered unto. This Ordinance is according to Institution to be applyed to visible Saints, though Unconverted, therefore it is for their saving good, and consequently for their conversion." [19] And he defined visible saints as "Such as make a serious profession of the true religion, together with those that do descend from them, till rejected of God." [20]

Stoddardeanism spread rapidly among the younger clergy and in the wealthier churches, in spite of the efforts of such influential opponents as the Mathers. These smug ministers of God still maintained their divine right to govern the affairs of the colony, though the revocation of the Massachusetts charter, in 1692, had put an official end to the theocracy. Cotton Mather's *Magnalia Christi Americana* was, even at the time of its publication in 1702, little more than a ponderous monument erected over a dead cause. Yet the

[19] Solomon Stoddard: *Appeal to the Learned,* p. 25.
[20] Stoddard: *Instituted Churches,* p. 6.

champions lingered on, apparently unaware of the moral and intellectual revolution going on about them. Cotton Mather, to be sure, made a desperate stand; he proposed to form Societies for the Reformation of Manners and for the Suppression of Vice. He outlined the following "Points of consideration, which may be read to the societies, at their meetings, from time to time, with a proper pause after each of them, that any member may offer what he pleases upon it. 1. Is there any remarkable disorder in the place, which requires our endeavours for the suppression of it? . . . 2. Is there any particular person, whose disorderly behaviour may be so scandalous, that it may be proper to send him our charitable admonition? Or, Are there any contending persons whom we should exhort to quench their contentions? 3. Is there any particular service to the interests of religion, which we may conveniently request our ministers to take notice of? 4. Is there anything which we may do well to mention and recommend to the magistrates, for the further promotion of good order? 5. Is there any sort of officers among us who are so unmindful of their duty, that we may properly remind them of it? 6. Can any further methods be devised that ignorance and wickedness may be chased from our people in general; and that domestic piety, in particular, may flourish among them? 7. Is there any instance of oppression or fraudulence in the dealings of any sort of people, which may call for our efforts to prevent it in future? 8. Is there any matter to be humbly recommended to the

93

legislative power, to be enacted into a law for the public benefit? 9. Do we know of any person languishing under heavy affliction, and what can we do for the succour of that afflicted neighbour? 10. Has any person a proposal to make, for the further advantage, assistance, and usefulness of this society?" [21]

This final attempt at universal prohibition was, of course, a vain effort to awaken in others a sense of sin which was quite lacking in the Mathers themselves. Being better than others, they tried in vain to make others better. In the end they became a laughingstock, entertaining the public by heaping invectives on their critics. Increase Mather died in 1723, and Cotton Mather in 1728, both sour old men, persecuted persecutors; and with them died the last and most pompous incarnations of the political theocracy.

The final blow at the Mather dynasty came from John Wise, and ushered in a new philosophy. Both the Rev. Colman, of Brattle Street, and the Rev. Stoddard, of Northampton, were conservative Presbyterians in the sense that they favored centralized church government, and the reforms which they advocated were in the interests of making the policies of the churches more palatable to an unregenerate generation of highly respectable laymen. They were quite willing to sacrifice the idea of the Holy Commonwealth for the sake of the prosperity of the churches. And nothing would have suited them better than a national church com-

[21] Cotton Mather: *Essays to Do Good* (Boston, 1710), pp. 132-3.

fortably established in the Commonwealth of New England.

From the very beginning of New England, however, there had been controversies between two theories of church government: between the Puritans (in the strict sense of the term) and the Separatists; the people of Massachusetts Bay and the pilgrims of Plymouth; the Barrowists and the Brownists; the Presbyterians and the Congregationalists; the aristocrats and the democrats. The issue now came to a head. Increase Mather had been one of those responsible for calling the Synod of 1679-80 to consider measures that "may appear necessary for the preventing of schisms, heresies, profaneness and the establishment of the churches in one faith and order of the gospel." [22] In 1691 he attempted a union of the New England churches with the Presbyterians. In 1700 the Massachusetts clergy, under the leadership of Solomon Stoddard, formed a plan for a "national church," and in 1705 they adopted a system of associations and standing councils. In 1708 the Connecticut clergy adopted the Saybrook Platform, which provided Consociations, or local presbyteries. A similar move was expected in Boston. This was the signal for revolt on the part of the strict Congregationalists. In 1710, John Wise, of the Second Church of Ipswich, published *The Churches Quarrel Espoused,* and in 1717, his famous *Vindication of the Government of the New England Churches.* These tracts might have been

[22] See Williston Walker: *A History of the Congregational Churches in the United States* (New York, 1894), p. 187.

merely restatements of the traditional Congregational theory, as it had been expressed in John Cotton's *Way of Congregational Churches Cleared,* or as it was restated later (1738) in Samuel Mather's *Apology for the Liberties of the Churches in New England*. But coming at this juncture, both the internal argument and the external application were radically changed. The other tracts were defenses of American churches against Anglican authority; John Wise's tracts were defenses of particular congregations against their own clergy. The conventional argument was based on the Dutch theology of primitive Christian democracy; John Wise's, on the ideas of natural law and civil liberty. The former Congregationalism was an integral part of the philosophy of the Holy Commonwealth; John Wise's Congregationalism was the first formulation of secular republicanism.

John Wise was no ordinary clergyman. He had been jailed for obstructing the collection of the royal taxes. He had been a fighting chaplain in the expedition against Quebec, and he later wrote a plea for paper currency. He had been contaminated, while at Harvard, by the new books in the library, and among them especially by Pufendorf's *De Iure Naturæ et Gentium;* and the legal theories which he gleaned from this work became the groundwork of his defense of democracy in the churches. "It seems most agreeable with the light of nature, that if there be any of the regular government settled in the church of God, it must needs be a democracy. This is a form of government which the light of nature does highly value, and often directs to as most agreeable to the just and natural prerogatives of human beings. . . . A man in making himself a subject, he alters himself from a freeman into a slave, which to do is repugnant to the law of nature. Also the natural equality of men amongst men must be duly favored; in that government was never established by God or nature, to give one man a prerogative to insult over another. . . . Honor all men. The end of all good government is to cultivate humanity, and promote the happiness of all, and the good of every man in all his rights, his life, liberty, estate, honor, etc., without injury or abuse done to any." [23] Then he goes on to prove that the New England congregations can be justified on the basis of these ideas.

Here we have a complete reversal of Puritan philosophy. The state is not justified because it makes a contribution to the Kingdom of God; the churches of God are justified because they tend to "cultivate humanity and promote the happiness of all and the good of every man in all his rights." Nothing could be a more eloquent tribute to the new spirit in New England: the churches are to be modelled on the principles of civil society, not *vice versa*. It is not the concept of democracy which is significant here, for that had been present from the beginning of New England; it is the secularization of democracy, the dethronement of God,

[23] John Wise: *Vindication of the Government of the New England Churches* (Boston, 1717), edition of 1860, pp. 54-5.

the unholiness of the commonwealth, that marks a revolution.

Had this been merely an attack on the Mathers and their Presbyterianism, the tract would have been buried with the Mathers; but, since it was really the beginning of a new religion, it was printed and reprinted, read and re-read, until by 1772 its re-publication transformed it into one of the bibles of the American Revolution. The Puritan sense of sin had yielded to what Samuel Mather called the liberty of the laity.

In these various ways the Puritan philosophy lost its hold on life in New England. The theory of the utter dependence of man on his sovereign God ceased to have any relevance to the facts of Puritan experience. Nevertheless it was not discarded. The preachers continued to preach it and the laymen continued to hear it; not because either of them believed it, but because they cherished it. Beliefs seldom become doubts; they become ritual. They become intrinsic parts of the social heritage, themes of public celebration. Thus the sense of sin became a genteel tradition, cherished in the imagination long after it had been surrendered in practice. The Puritan insistence on human depravity became the compensatory justification of Yankee moral complacency.

If you wish a concrete picture of this situation, imagine yourself seated in the Old South Church of Boston, on a Sunday about the year 1724, listening to the pastor, the Reverend Mr. Samuel Willard, Vice-President of

Harvard College, while he preaches one of his two hundred and fifty *Expository Lectures on the Assembly's
Shorter Catechism*. You are surrounded by a congregation of very dignified and prosperous Bostonians.
They are the elect, and acknowledge no superiors on
earth; for the King of England, though he is formally
and distantly acknowledged by them as their sovereign,
is not their moral superior either in their own eyes or
in the sight of their real ruler, the Lord of heaven and
earth. To these favored few of the Lord, the Reverend
Willard is expounding the first question of the catechism, which is, I suppose, the first question absolutely,
—"What is the chief end of man?"

"Answer: Man's chief end is to glorify God, and enjoy Him forever. . . . If we could speak exactly there
is but One of these, viz. to glorify God, which is man's
chief end; the other is immediately subordinated. . . .
It is man's duty to seek his own best good, which consists in enjoying of God; but he is to do it in and for
the Glory of God. . . .

"The object of man's happiness is out of himself
Man cannot be his own felicity. He is a dependent
creature; his being and his blessedness are two things.
He cannot dwell at home. He doth not enjoy in himself a self-sufficiency. . . . Neither can the body or soul
be at rest, till they meet with and fall upon an object
that may give them satisfaction. This is it that hath
made the whole world a company of seekers asking for
Good . . .

"The whole creation affords no such object, the fruition whereof can make a man happy. . . . There are three defects in the creature, rendring it insufficient for our perfect well-being. (1) Its unsuitableness. If there were enough of it, yet it is not accommodated to all a man's wants; nay, those which are his greatest wants and make him truly miserable. . . . (2) Its scantiness. Were it never so suitable, yet there is not enough of it. The reaches of a man's soul are so vast, that they can grasp in the whole creation and scarce feel it. The desire of man, that horseleeches daughter, is still crying Give, Give. The bed is too narrow, and the covering too short. The world looks bulky but it is empty, void and waste. Many have had too much, but never yet any had enough. . . . (3) Its short continuance and uncertainty. Man is a creature made for perpetuity, and if his object be not stable, and durable, it will sooner or later leave him under horrible disappointment, and so will these things. They are broken cisterns. They are certain in nothing but uncertainty. . . . How then can they make a man happy?

"God and He only is such an object, in the enjoyment of whom, there is perfect satisfaction and blessedness. . . . Every action in a man's life that doth not serve to this great end is a vain action. . . . There are but a few that know what they were made for. . . . The greatest number of the children of men live in vain." [24]

[24] Samuel Willard: *A Compleat Body of Divinity, in 250 expository lectures on the Assembly's Shorter Catechism, wherein the doctrines of the Christian religion are unfolded, their truth confirmed, their excellence displayed, their usefulness improved; contrary errors and vices refuted and*

LOSS OF THE SENSE OF SIN

Unless you are exceptionally irresponsive, the boundless imagination and occasional eloquence of the preacher has touched you. Your soul expands until it can grasp the whole creation and scarcely feel it. The world looks empty, void and waste, full of horrible disappointments and broken cisterns. You turn, therefore, for your own best good and enjoyment to the glory of God and in him you dwell at home. But now church is over, and you are plunged into the heart of Boston, the metropolis of New England, growing, enterprising, exciting, absorbing. It is not empty, void or waste. God himself must find his own best good and enjoyment in dwelling at home in Boston!

Some such intellectual somersault every Bostonian performed every Sunday, and, though an apparently difficult feat, it was soon performed with great facility. No habit, in fact, is more easily formed than this, of divorcing the world of imagination from the world of action. It is an easy way out of a serious predicament. Both body and conscience are satisfied and neither at the expense of the other. On Sunday the Puritan as whole-heartedly lost himself in God as on Monday he devoted himself to business. The infinite cravings of the Puritan conscience could feed on the infinite glory of God, while that other "horse-leeche's daughter," the desires of the body, could feast on the abundant wealth of the Atlantic Ocean and the virgin forests and fields of a new continent.

exposed, objections answered, controversies settled, cases of conscience resolved, and a great light thereby reflected on the present age (Boston, 1726), pp. 1, 4, 8.

CHAPTER IV

THE GREAT AWAKENING

When, in 1727, the Reverend Mr. Stoddard of North-ampton, being then in his eighty-fourth year, asked his grandson, Jonathan Edwards, to become his assist-ant and successor, he little dreamed that this sickly, scholarly youth would become a formidable foe of Stoddardeanism and the most powerful exponent of the old Puritan faith ever produced in New England. Northampton, though a frontier town, was one of the most aristocratic and prosperous communities outside of Boston, being the county-seat of the largest and most fertile county in Massachusetts. For over twenty years Stoddard had here been practicing openly his liberal principles regarding church membership, and for an even longer period he had tacitly compromised with the unregenerate. The church was consequently prosperous and influential; there was a reigning spirit of peace and good fellowship among the people. To mention but one instance of the genial quality of this society, it had become customary in New England to celebrate the Sabbath from sun-down on Saturday to sun-down on Sunday, and this had given rise, espe-cially in Northampton, to celebrating the close of the religious services by company-keeping on Sunday evenings; the various families of the church would call on each other, and the young folks went so far as to keep company without the rest of the family. In short, it was a very agreeable and refined society into which young Edwards was called. His grandfather's good standing made it easy for him to gain access, and his own quiet, pious manner soon made him a popular favorite. To cap it all, when, shortly after his arrival, Edwards married Miss Pierrepont, an unusually beautiful girl of seventeen from one of the best families of New Haven, the venerable old Stoddard had every reason to die happy and rest in peace.

The first warning of impending trouble came in 1731, when Edwards was asked to deliver a sermon in Boston. This was not an ordinary Sunday service, it was a social event: Boston was paying its respects to Northampton. On this occasion the young preacher greeted his congregation with the following words: "What God aims at in the disposition of things in the affair of redemption is that man should not glory in himself, but alone in God; That no flesh should glory in his presence,—that according as it is written, He that glorieth, let him glory in the Lord." [1]

Courageously and thoroughly he developed the doctrine that God is glorified by man's entire dependence, and he closed his lecture with the words: "Let us be exhorted to exalt God alone, and ascribe to him all the

[1] Jonathan Edwards: *Sermon VI; God Glorified in Man's Dependence* (1731). In Dr. Sereno Edwards Dwight (Editor): *The Works of President Edwards with a Memoir of His Life* (New York, 1829), Vol. VII, p. 149. Subsequent citations refer to this edition.

glory of redemption. Let us endeavour to obtain, and increase in, a sensibleness of our great dependence on God, to have our eye on him alone, to mortify a self-dependent, and self-righteous disposition. Man is naturally prone to exalt himself, and depend on his own power or goodness; as though from himself he must expect happiness. He is prone to have respect to enjoyments alien from God and his Spirit, as those in which happiness is to be found.—But this doctrine should teach us to exalt God *alone;* as by trust and reliance, so by praise. Let him that glorieth, glory in the Lord. Hath any man hope that he is converted, and sanctified, and that his mind is endowed with true excellency and spiritual beauty? that his sins are forgiven, and he received into God's favour, and exalted to the honour and blessedness of being his child, and an heir of eternal life? let him give God all the glory; who alone makes him to differ from the worst of men in this world, or the most miserable of the damned in hell. Hath any man much comfort and strong hope of eternal life? let not his hope lift him up, but dispose him the more to abase himself, to reflect on his own exceeding unworthiness of such a favour, and to exalt God alone. Is any man eminent in holiness, and abundant in good works? let him take nothing of the glory of it to himself, but ascribe it to him whose 'workmanship we are, created in Christ Jesus unto good works.'" [2]

The sermon created a sensation, and Edwards imme-

[2] Vol. VII, p. 162.

diately became the center of attention. Several ministers had the sermon printed, commending its young author as "a workman that needs not to be ashamed before his brethren," and praising "those who assert and maintain these evangelical principles," and rejoicing "that our churches (notwithstanding all their degeneracies) have still a high value for such principles, and for those who publicly own and teach them." [3] Such comments, however, do not conceal the disquieting effect which the sermon had. Here was a young man who still preached doctrines which even the older clergy regarded as old-fashioned, and which in any other mouth would have sounded hypocritical. But coming from him, they were not mere reassertions of traditional themes; they came with a logical vigor and an intimate meaning which gave them a strangely new quality. He was not an orator; he confined himself rather closely to his manuscript, leaned on one elbow, and used no gestures. His voice was thin, almost effeminate. Nevertheless all who heard him were not only irresistibly attracted to him, but profoundly influenced by his ideas.

The secret of Edwards' power lay probably in the fact that the gospel he preached was primarily neither a product of scholastic and theological learning nor a philosophical reflection on the general moral problems of his time; it was a fruit of his own inner struggles. He was unusually learned, to be sure, and his sermons

[3] Vol. VII, p. 148. *Advertisement to the Reader Respecting the First Sermon,* by T. Prince and W. Cooper (1731).

were constructed like academic theses; he was skilled in argument and took an active part in the controversies of his day; but underneath his learning and his dialectical skill, there was a direct, personal acquaintance knowledge. In Jonathan Edwards religion was essentially a kind of private experience; he succeeded in doing what Anne Hutchinson had in a manner unsuccessfully attempted. For in New England, ever since the defeat of the familists, religion had been an objective social institution, preoccupied with public concerns; Edwards, however, transformed it into an inner discipline of the emotions. The gospel of the divine sovereignty, of election, of predestination, and of the Covenant of Grace, which the New England Puritans had constructed into a social and political philosophy, was now transferred to the inner life of the soul.

Edwards was surprisingly blind to the political philosophy of the Holy Commonwealth. Though he was preoccupied with a *History of Redemption* (published in 1739), which went over the familiar ground of the Christian philosophers of history from Saint Augustine to Cotton Mather, and which would have given him ample opportunity to develop the Puritan political theory, he nowhere mentions it. He does not even attempt a refutation. He gives a passing reference to New England in connection with the spread of the Kingdom of God among the heathen, but the whole plan of the work minimizes the historical significance of the New England theocracy. The theocracy was dead and Edwards apparently saw the practical futility of the political philosophy which it had generated. But, though it had failed in its social application, this same doctrine contained also a private and personal meaning, a meaning which had been submerged during the period of prevailingly public concerns, but which now rapidly came to the surface in the minds of those whole-hearted and thoroughgoing Puritans who continued to take the doctrine seriously in spite of its political irrelevancy. After all, they reflected, "the Kingdom of God is *within* you." God claims an absolute sovereignty over each human soul, which being thus entirely dependent on him, is in itself insignificant and achieves value only in so far as it reflects his glory. This essential doctrine of Calvinism still pervaded the popular mind though it had lost its social significance, and it was upon this surviving foundation of Calvinistic ideas that Edwards built his personal philosophy as well as that profound revival of Puritanism known as the Great Awakening.

The story of how Edwards attained this insight must be told in his own words: "From my childhood up, my mind had been full of objections against the doctrine of God's sovereignty, in choosing whom he would to eternal life, and rejecting whom he pleased; leaving them eternally to perish, and be everlastingly tormented in hell. It used to appear like a horrible doctrine to me. But I remember the time very well, when I seemed to be convinced, and fully satisfied, as to this sovereignty of God, and his justice in thus eternally disposing of men, according to his sovereign pleasure. But never could give an account, how, or by what means, I was thus convinced, not in the least imagining at the time, nor a long time after, that there was any extraordinary influence of God's Spirit in it; but only that now I saw further, and my reason apprehended the justice and reasonableness of it. However, my mind rested in it; and it put an end to all those cavils and objections. And there has been a wonderful alteration in my mind, with respect to the doctrine of God's sovereignty, from that day to this; so that I scarce ever have found so much as the rising of an objection against it, in the most absolute sense, in God shewing mercy to whom he will shew mercy, and hardening whom he will. God's absolute sovereignty and justice, with respect to salvation and damnation is what my mind seems to rest assured of, as much as of any thing that I see with my eyes; at least it is so at times. But I have often since that first conviction, had quite another sense of God's sovereignty than I had then. I have often since had not only a conviction, but a *delightful* conviction. The doctrine has very often appeared exceedingly pleasant, bright, and sweet. Absolute sovereignty is what I love to ascribe to God. But my first conviction was not so.

"The first instance, that I remember, of that sort of inward, sweet delight in God and divine things, that I have lived much in since, was on reading those words, I Tim. i. 17. *Now unto the King eternal, immortal, invisible, the only wise God, be honour and glory for ever' and ever. Amen.* As I read the words, there came into my soul, and was as it were diffused through it, a sense of the glory of the Divine Being; a new sense, quite different from any thing I ever experienced before. Never any words of Scripture seemed to me as these words did. I thought with myself, how excellent a Being that was, and how happy I should be, if I might enjoy that God, and be rapt up to him in heaven, and be as it were swallowed up in him for ever! I kept saying, and as it were singing, over these words of scripture to myself; and went to pray to God that I might enjoy him, and prayed in a manner quite different from what I used to do; with a new sort of affection. But it never came into my thought, that there was any thing spiritual or of a saving nature in this.

"From about that time, I began to have a new kind of apprehensions and ideas of Christ, and the work of redemption, and the glorious way of salvation by him. An inward, sweet sense of these things, at times, came into my heart; and my soul was led away in pleasant views and contemplations of them. . . .

"This I know not how to express otherwise, than by a calm, sweet abstraction of soul from all the concerns of this world; and sometimes a kind of vision, or fixed ideas and imaginations, of being alone in the mountains, or some solitary wilderness, far from all mankind, sweetly conversing with Christ, and wrapt and swallowed up in God. The sense I had of divine things, would often of a sudden kindle up, as it were, a sweet burning in my heart; an ardour of soul, that I know not how to express.

"After this my sense of divine things gradually increased, and became more and more lively, and had more of that inward sweetness. The appearance of everything was altered; there seemed to be, as it were, a calm, sweet, cast, or appearance of divine glory, in almost everything. God's excellency, his wisdom, his purity and love, seemed to appear in every thing; in the sun, moon, and stars; in the clouds and blue sky; in the grass, flowers, trees; in the water, and all nature; which used greatly to fix my mind. I often used to sit and view the moon for a long time; and in the day, spent much time in viewing the clouds and sky, to behold the sweet glory of God in these things: in the meantime, singing forth, with a low voice, my contemplations of the Creator and Redeemer. . . .

"I felt then great satisfaction, as to my good estate; but that did not content me. I had vehement longings of soul after God and Christ, and after more holiness, wherewith my heart seemed to be full, and ready to break; which often brought to my mind the words of the Psalmist, Psal. cxix. 28. *My soul breaketh for the longing it hath.* I often felt a mourning and lamenting in my heart, that I had not turned to God sooner, that I might have had more time to grow in grace. My mind was greatly fixed on divine things; almost perpetually in the contemplation of them. I spent most of my time in thinking of divine things, year after year; often walking alone in the woods, and solitary places, for meditation, soliloquy, and prayer, and converse with God; and it was always my manner, at such times, to sing forth my contemplations. I was almost constantly in ejaculatory prayer, wherever I was. Prayer seemed to be natural to me, as the breath by which the inward burnings of my heart had vent. The delights which I now felt in the things of religion, were of an exceedingly different kind from those before-mentioned, that I had when a boy; and what then I had no more notion of, than one born blind has of pleasant and beautiful colours. They were of a more inward, pure, soul-animating and refreshing nature. Those former delights never reached the heart; and did not arise from any sight of the divine excellency of the things of God; or any taste of the soul-satisfying and life-giving good there is in them." [4]

This account was written by Edwards considerably later in life and is evidently in part a rationalization of his experience. Nevertheless, the truth of its main outlines is borne out by his diary and resolutions, written while he was undergoing the experiences here described. The fundamental point is clear enough: Edwards had interpreted the doctrine of God's sovereignty to mean that the whole of his life should be continually dominated by God. This was the individual analogue of the theocracy. And it was no less stormy. The wars of the Lord in the soul of Jonathan Edwards were as intense as the wars of the Lord in New England, and

---

[4] Vol. I, pp. 60-2. "Found among his papers . . . written near twenty years afterwards, for his own private benefit" (Vol. I, p. 58).

Edwards' *Journal* should be read as a companion-piece to Mather's *Magnalia*. In the end, however, the Lord did achieve a sovereignty in him such as he seldom achieves in a human soul, and as he certainly never achieved in New England society, even in the holiest days of the Holy Commonwealth.

In his childhood, Edwards enjoyed his religion as he did any other natural good of life. He tells how he and his playmates used to play at religion, just as they played at ball. They "built a booth in a swamp, in a very retired spot, for a place of prayer." [5] He used to pray five times a day and had particular secret places in the woods where he "was from time to time much affected." On such occasions he "seemed to be in his element." But this was mere childish delight, or, as Edwards called it, self-righteous pleasure in religious practices, and not an exhibition of grace at all, for God is not merely one of the natural delights of the soul, he is Lord of all. All things are seen in relation to God, and all are irradiated by his glory. Edwards believed literally that his whole life ought to be continually preoccupied with matters of religion, and in order to make this possible, he tried to make of every experience a religious experience. Some of his efforts in this direction are pathetic. Though he soon attained complete assurance of his justification before God and revelled in the sweetness of God's sovereignty, he had periods of religious depression which caused him much concern. Especially during his

[5] Vol. I, p. 59.

tutorship at Yale, when the burden of sharing in the administration of the college necessarily demanded his attention to mundane matters, he complained of being "in a low, sunk estate and condition, miserably senseless . . . about spiritual things." It was physically impossible for him to keep himself emotionally keyed up to the pitch he demanded, and even though he was absolutely convinced that God had shed his free grace upon him, he was never without concern for his spiritual estate. He prolonged his meditations by writing them in a booklet which he kept near him in order that when he found his mind wandering he might re-read his own reflections. Here are some typical passages from his diary:

"Now, henceforth, I am not to act, in any respect, as my own. I shall act as my own, if I ever make use of any of my powers, to any thing, that is not to the glory of God, and do not make the glorifying of him, my whole and entire business; if I murmur in the least at affliction; if I grieve at the prosperity of others; if I am in any way uncharitable; if I am angry, because of injuries; if I revenge them; if I do any thing, purely to please myself, or if I avoid any thing, for the sake of my own ease; if I omit any thing, because it is great self-denial; if I trust to myself, if I take any of the praise of any good that I do, or that God doth by me; or if I am in any way proud. This day, made the 42d and 43d Resolutions:—Whether or no, any other end ought to have any influence at all, on any of my actions; or, whether any action ought to be any otherwise, in any respect, than it would be, if nothing else but religion had the least influence on my mind. Wherefore, I make the 44th Resolution.

"Query: Whether any delight, or satisfaction, ought to be allowed, because any other end is obtained, beside a religious one. In the afternoon, I answer, Yes; because, if we should never suffer ourselves to rejoice, but because we have obtained a religious end, we should never rejoice at the sight of friends, we should not allow ourselves any pleasure in our food, whereby the animal spirits would be withdrawn, and good digestion hindered. But the query is to be answered thus:—We never ought to allow any joy or sorrow, but what helps religion. Wherefore, I make the 45th Resolution. . . .

"*At night.* This week, the weekly account rose higher than ordinary. It is suggested to me, that too constant a mortification, and too vigorous application to religion, may be prejudicial to health; but nevertheless I will plainly feel it and experience it, before I cease on this account. It is no matter how much tired and weary I am, if my health is not impaired." [6]

"*Tuesday, Sept.* 2. By a sparingness in diet, and eating as much as may be, what is light and easy of digestion, I shall doubtless be able to think more clearly, and shall gain time; 1. By lengthening out my life; 2. Shall need less time for digestion, after meals; 3. Shall be able to study more closely, without injury to my

[6] Vol. I, pp. 79-80. Diary, Jan. 12, 1723.

health; 4. Shall need less time for sleep; 5. Shall more seldom be troubled with the head-ache.

"*Wednesday, Sept.* 30. It has been a prevailing thought with me, to which I have given place in practice, that it is best, sometimes, to eat or drink, when it will do me no good, because the hurt, that it will do me, will not be equal, to the trouble of denying myself. But I have determined, to suffer that thought to prevail no longer. The hurries of commencement, and diversion of the vacancy, has been the occasion of my sinking so exceedingly, as in the three last weeks." [7]

Similarly he regarded his love for Sarah Pierrepont as but one episode in his love of God: "They say there is a young lady in (New Haven) who is beloved of that Great Being, who made and rules the world, and that there are certain seasons in which this Great Being, in some way or other invisible, comes to her and fills her mind with exceeding sweet delights, and that she hardly cares for any thing, except to meditate on him— that she expects after a while to be received up where he is, to be raised up out of the world and caught up into heaven; being assured that he loves her too well to let her remain at a distance from him always. There she is to dwell with him, and to be ravished with his love and delight forever. Therefore, if you present all the world before her, with the richest of its treasures, she disregards it and cares not for it, and is unmindful of any pain or affliction. She has a strange sweetness in her mind, and singular purity in her affections; is most

[7] Vol. I, p. 104. Diary, 1724.

just and conscientious in all her conduct; and you could not persuade her to do any thing wrong or sinful, if you would give her all the world, lest she should offend this Great Being. She is of a wonderful sweetness, calmness and universal benevolence of mind; especially after this Great God has manifested himself to her mind. She will sometimes go about from place to place, singing sweetly; and seems to be always full of joy and pleasure; and no one knows for what. She loves to be alone, walking in the fields and groves, and seems to have someone invisible always conversing with her." [8]

The culmination, as well as the fundamental paradox of this whole self-discipline, is revealed in the following passage:

"I have greatly longed of late, for a broken heart, and to lie low before God; and, when I ask for humility, I cannot bear the thoughts of being no more humble than other christians. It seems to me, that though their degrees of humility may be suitable for them, yet it would be a vile self-exaltation in me, not to be the lowest in humility of all mankind. Others speak of their longing to be 'humbled to the dust'; that may be a proper expression for them, but I always think of myself, that I ought, and it is an expression that has long been natural for me to use in prayer, 'to lie infinitely low before God.' . . . And yet, I am greatly afflicted with a proud and self-righteous spirit, much more sensibly than I used to be formerly. I see that

[8] Vol. I, pp. 114-5. "Written on a blank leaf, in 1723."

serpent rising and putting forth its head continually,
every where, all around me." [9]

Whether Jonathan Edwards was really the humblest
sinner in Christendom, and really subjected all his interests to the divine sovereignty; or whether he merely
found a pious terminology for all the secular passions
which he really vented on secular objects; or whether
these two are merely different ways of saying the same
thing, is still an unsolved problem. But whatever the
motives which drove him to God, whether poetry, or
sex, or an inferiority complex, or a superiority complex,
or *Weltschmerz,* or all of these, the fact remains that
in his mind these were all aspects of a single concern,
and that the sovereignty of God was an all-pervasive
and all-inclusive object of love. He lived out completely in his own soul the whole Puritan philosophy,
and became absolutely convinced on the basis of his
own experience that the doctrine was sound. In everything he saw God's glory, and in the sweetness of this
glory he found salvation for his miserable soul.

The preaching which grew out of such intense con-
centration of emotion, imagination and will, naturally
was itself intense and vibrant with personal meaning.
Its effects soon made themselves felt. The sensation
created in Boston was merely a symptom of what was
taking place in Northampton. Even during Stoddard's
time there had been occasional waves of religious attention, as they were called, and mild revivals were by

[9] Vol. I, p. 135. Written about 1740.

no means unknown in New England. But what now took place was unprecedented. It was not merely that an increasing number of people became interested in the church, nor even that increasing numbers each year professed conversion and owned the Covenant; it was rather that everybody soon became preoccupied with the salvation of his soul. Imagine the doubts and terrors which haunted the minds of those who were less certain than Edwards that a supernatural gift of grace had been bestowed on them, and the emotional tension which the great majority of the congregation felt when they asked themselves: "Have I absolute proof?" It must be remembered that this was not a moral problem, in the sense that it concerned the secular good-will and conduct or even the sincere seeking for salvation. Such miserable seeking was of no avail and merely made matters worse. Salvation must come from above; it was God's doing. Man can but wait upon the Lord. This waiting was, however, no passive resignation to fate; it was an anxious expectancy of the visible signs of God's operations. God was regarded as a sort of spiritual volcano, who when once active might be expected to send down overwhelming showers of the holy fire. Consequently, as soon as evidences of the workings of God's grace began to appear, everyone was thrown into a panic. There was a local disturbance in Northampton from 1734 to 1737, which seemed to subside a little during the next few years, when suddenly in 1740 not only Northampton but all New England was set on fire by The Great

Awakening. From Edwards' own account of this movement we take the following:

"The spirit of God began extraordinarily to set in, and wonderfully to work amongst us; and there were, very suddenly, one after another, five or six persons, who were to all appearance savingly converted, and some of them wrought upon in a very remarkable manner.

"Particularly, I was surprised with the relation of a young woman, who had been one of the greatest company-keepers in the whole town. When she came to me, I had never heard that she was become in any wise serious, but by the conversation I then had with her, it appeared to me, that what she gave an account of, was a glorious work of God's infinite power and sovereign grace; and that God had given her a new heart, truly broken and sanctified. . . .

"Presently upon this, a great and earnest concern about the great things of religion, and the eternal world, became universal in all parts of the town, and among persons of all degrees, and all ages. The noise amongst the dry bones waxed louder and louder; all other talk but about spiritual and eternal things was soon thrown by; all the conversation, in all companies and upon all occasions, was upon these things only, unless so much as was necessary for people carrying on their ordinary secular business. Other discourse than of the things of religion, would scarcely be tolerated in any company. The minds of people were wonderfully taken off from the world, it was treated amongst us as a thing of very little consequence. They seemed to follow their worldly business, more as a part of their duty, than from any disposition they had to it; the temptation now seemed to lie on that hand, to neglect worldly affairs too much, and to spend too much time in the immediate exercise of religion. . . .

"But although people did not ordinarily neglect their worldly business; yet Religion was with all sorts the great concern, and the world was a thing only by the bye. The only thing in their view was to get the kingdom of heaven, and everyone appeared pressing into it. The engagedness of their hearts in this great concern could not be hid, it appeared in their very countenances. It then was a dreadful thing amongst us to lie out of Christ, in danger every day of dropping into hell; and what persons minds were intent upon, was to escape for their lives, and to fly from the wrath to come. . . .

"Our young people when they met, were wont to spend the time in talking of the excellency and dying love of Jesus Christ, the glory of the way of salvation, the wonderful, free, and sovereign grace of God, his glorious work in the conversion of a soul, the truth and certainty of the great things of God's word, the sweetness of the views of his perfections, &c. And even at weddings, which formerly were mere occasions of mirth and jollity, there was now no discourse of any thing but religion, and no appearance of any but spiritual mirth. Those amongst us who had been formerly converted, were greatly enlivened, and renewed with fresh and extraordinary incomes of the spirit of God; though some much more than others, according to the measure of the gift of Christ. Many who before had laboured under difficulties about their own state, had now their doubts removed by more satisfying experience, and more clear discoveries of God's love. . . .

"In the month of March, the people in South-Hadley began to be seized with deep concern about the things of religion; which very soon became universal. . . . About the same time, it began to break forth in the west part of Suffield, (where it also has been very great) and it soon spread into all parts of the town. It next appeared at Sunderland, and soon overspread the town; and I believe was for a season not less remarkable than it was here. About the same time it began to appear in a part of Deerfield, called Green River, and afterwards filled the town, and there has been a glorious work there. It began also to be manifest in the south part of Hatfield, in a place called the Hill, and the whole town, in the second week in April, seemed to be seized, as it were at once, with concern about the things of religion; and the work of God had been great there. There has been also a very general awakening at West-Springfield and Long Meadow; and in Enfield there was for a time a pretty general concern amongst some who before had been very loose persons. About the same time that this appeared at Enfield, the Rev. Mr. Bull of Westfield, informed me, that there had been a great alteration there, and that more had been done in one week than in seven years before. Something of this work likewise appeared in the first precinct in Springfield, principally in the north and south extremes of the parish. And in Hadley old town, there gradually appeared so much of a work of God on souls, as at another time would have been thought worthy of much notice. For a short time there was also a very great and general concern of the like nature at Northfield. . . .

"This remarkable pouring out of the Spirit of God, which thus extended from one end to the other of this country, was not confined to it, but many places in Connecticut have partaken in the same mercy." [10]

From Connecticut it spread into eastern Massachusetts and into northern New Jersey. Soon it was of such dimensions that neither Edwards nor any group of ministers could control it. It was clearly a work of God. In September of 1740, George Whitefield arrived in New England. His preaching, which had already caused a stir in other colonies and in England, now fanned the revival to fever heat. Bodily effects, such as screamings, faintings, convulsions, and other symptoms of hysteria, became common. The evil effects became so alarming that soon no one could tell whether it was God or the devil who was most active. The devil, of course, would not be caught napping. "Satan," said Whitefield, "now begins to throw many

[10] Vol. IV, pp. 21, 22, 24, 25. *A Faithful Narrative of the Surprising Work of God, in the Conversion of Many Hundred Souls, in Northampton, and the Neighbouring towns and Villages of New-Hampshire, in New England. In a letter to the Rev. Dr. Colman of Boston.* Written Nov. 6, 1736; published London, 1737.

into fits." [11] Those who disliked the wave of "enthusiasm" began to regard the whole movement as a work of the devil. President Chauncy, of Harvard, attacked it vigorously. At Yale several students were denied their diplomas because of their "enthusiasm." Not only the universities, but also the more sober and worldly people of the coastal cities in general disapproved of it. On the other hand, there was evidently a large number of genuine conversions, and even of the fits many seemed to be works of God. The attitude generally taken toward the movement was either one of violent denunciation, or one of undiscriminating acceptance; few persons attempted a more reflective evaluation.

Finally Edwards, alarmed at the growing confusion, excitement and insanity, undertook the difficult task of determining the "distinguishing marks of a work of the spirit of God," a task which led to his *Thoughts on the Revival of 1740* and to the more elaborate *Treatise on the Religious Affections*. There is no greater proof of Edwards' intellectual ability than this cool, critical analysis, written in the midst of a wave of religious frenzy for which the author himself was largely responsible. Perhaps it was his feeling of responsibility for the movement which led him to make this attempt to control it. In opposition to the conservatives, he maintained that religion was primarily a matter of the affections; in opposition to the extreme

[11] Joseph Tracy: *The Great Awakening: A History of the Revival of Religion in the time of Edwards and Whitefield* (Boston, 1842), p. 224.

enthusiasts, he emphasized the necessity of a critical attitude toward the affections. The great majority of the current disturbances he listed as no sign either that the affections are, or are not, truly gracious. It is no sign, for instance, one way or the other, that religious affections are very great or raised very high, that they have great effects on the body (such as trembling, groaning, being sick, crying out, panting and fainting), that they cause those who have them to be fluent, fervent and abundant in talking of religious things, that persons did not excite them by their own endeavors, that they come to the mind in a remarkable manner with texts of Scripture, that there is an appearance of love in them, that comforts and joys seem to follow in a certain order, that they may much dispose persons with their mouths to praise and glorify God, that they make persons exceeding confident, or that the relations persons give of them are very affecting. The chief sign, on the other hand, both to ourselves and to others that they are of divine origin is that "their fruit is Christian practice." "Neither a longing after great discoveries, or after great tastes of the love of God, nor longing to be in heaven, nor longing to die, are in any measure so distinguishing marks of true saints, as longing after a more holy heart, and living a more holy life." [12]

The effect of these writings was not what Edwards had intended it to be. He expected them to contribute to the increased cultivation of the religious affections,

[12] Vol. V, pp. 252-3. *A Treatise Concerning Religious Affections* (1746).

in the same way that he himself had made holiness, or Christian practice, his constant preoccupation, "so that it may be said, not only to be his business at certain seasons, the business of Sabbath-days, or certain extraordinary times, or the business of a month, or a year, or of seven years, or his business under certain circumstances; but the *business of his life.*" [13]   But for most readers these writings, coming as they did when the reaction to the revival had already set in, the emphasis on Christian practice had the effect of discounting the affections and of turning their attention to the more secular and overt aspects of conduct.   In short, Edwards' own critical attitude, combined with the current excesses, encouraged in many a sceptical attitude toward the whole period of emotional tension, and even toward the whole philosophy of God's outpourings of grace.   Consequently, with the return to religious normalcy, there came a general feeling of relief and relaxation.   The Great Awakening proved to be very temporary.   Desperate means seldom accomplish permanent results.   Certainly an atmosphere of emotional tension is of necessity a transitory phase of human experience; it is physiologically impossible to live long on that level.   When the inevitable reaction came, it left the Puritan philosophy in a much more precarious position than ever, since the next generation not only failed to see its force, but was in addition taught to be more cautious and cool in its religious affections.   New England, instead of making religion the

[13] Vol. V, p. 253.

business of life, gladly returned to the life of business, and has ever since kept itself comparatively aloof from great awakenings. These revivals took their course westward and southward.

Edwards, however, did not share in this general disillusion. His imagination had been kindled and he saw this revival in the perspective of the great themes of Christian history. It dawned on him that perhaps God in these latter times was beginning that final work of human redemption which was to overthrow the Anti-Christ, and usher in the Kingdom of God. Perhaps New England, after all, was designed for the peculiar manifestation of God's glory. Perhaps just when New England was abandoning the wars of the Lord, the Lord himself was taking a hand in the contest, and was now establishing by supernatural means that Holy Commonwealth which had been the dream of the Puritan imagination. "Not by the sword, but by the outpouring of my Holy Spirit" kept ringing in Edwards' ears. Not by political power, nor by ecclesiastical policy, but by the immediate diffusion of God's grace in the hearts of the people, the Lord was bringing to pass that great purpose to which New England was dedicated and which the proud politicians, trusting in their swords rather than in the grace of God, had almost brought to ruin. God, indeed, was exercising his absolute sovereignty and was demonstrating to all the world that he is able to rule the hearts of men when all human efforts fail.

This revival, therefore, according to Edwards, was

but the "preparatory, which prepares the way for Christ's coming to destroy the kingdom of antichrist, and to set up his own kingdom in the world. . . . It is to be hoped, a far more pure, extensive, and glorious revival of religion is not far off, which will more properly be the beginning of that work which in its issue shall overthrow the kingdom of antichrist, and of Satan through the world." [14]

"If we consider how long since the things foretold as what should precede this great event, have been accomplished; and how long this event has been expected by the Church of God, and thought to be nigh by the most eminent men of God, in the church; and withal consider what the state of things now is, and has for a considerable time been, in the church of God, and the world of mankind; we cannot reasonably think otherwise, than that the beginning of this great work of God must be near. And there are many things that make it probable that this work will begin in America. . . .

"God has made as it were two worlds here below, two great habitable continents, far separated one from the other; The latter is as it were not but newly created; it has been, till of late, wholly the possession of Satan, the church of God having never been in it, as it has been in the other continent, from the beginning of the world. This new world is probably now discovered,

[14] Vol. III, pp. 538-9. *An Humble Attempt to promote Explicit Agreement and Visible Union of God's People in Extraordinary Prayer for the Revival of Religion and the Advancement of Christ's Kingdom on Earth* (1747).

that the new and most glorious state of God's church on earth might commence there; that God might in it begin a new world in a spiritual respect, when he creates the new heavens and new earth.

"God has already put that honour upon the other continent, that Christ was born there literally, and there made the 'purchase of redemption.' So, as Providence observes a kind of equal distribution of things, it is not unlikely that the great spiritual birth of Christ, and the most glorious 'application of redemption,' is to begin in this. . . .

"Now as when God is about to do some great work for his church, his manner is to begin at the lower end; so, when he is about to renew the whole habitable earth, it is probable that he will begin in this utmost, meanest, youngest and weakest part of it, where the church of God has been planted last of all; and so the first shall be last, and the last first; and that will be fulfilled in an eminent manner in Isa. xxiv. 19. 'From the uttermost part of the earth have we heard songs, even glory to the righteous.' " [15]

With this new version of the philosophy of the Holy Commonwealth in mind, and with the number of the elect greatly swelled by the revival, Jonathan Edwards was encouraged to attempt once more the purification of the churches. Thanks to the wonderful works of saving grace, the churches could at last be both pure and powerful. It no longer seemed impossible to insist

[15] Vol. IV, pp. 128-9, 131-2. *Some Thoughts Concerning the Present Revival of Religion in New England, and the Way in which it ought to be acknowledged and promoted* (1742).

that only the regenerate be admitted to the communion. Accordingly, in 1746, Edwards came out boldly with his *Humble Inquiry into the Rules of the Word of God, concerning the Qualifications requisite to a Complete Standing and Full Communion in the Visible Christian Church,* in which, after due apologies to his grandfather and repeated appeals to the candid reflection and impartial judgment of his congregation, he reasserted the strict theory of the Church Covenant.

"The practice of promiscuous admission—or that way of taking all into the church indifferently, as visible saints, who are not either ignorant or scandalous—and at the same time that custom taking place of persons publishing their own conversion in common conversation; where these two things meet together, they unavoidably make two distinct kinds of visible churches, or different bodies of professing saints, one within another, openly distinguished one from another, as it were by a visible dividing line. One company consisting of those who are visibly gracious Christians, and open professors of godliness; another consisting of those who are visibly moral livers, and only profess common virtues, without pretending to any special and spiritual experiences in their hearts, and who therefore are not reputed to be converts. I may appeal to those acquainted with the state of the churches, whether this be not actually the case in some, where this method of proceeding has been long established. But I leave the judicious reader to make his own remarks on this case, and to determine, whether there be a just foundation in scripture or reason for any such state of things; which to me, I confess, carries the face of glaring absurdity." [16]

Edwards had begun to act on this theory several years before, but without serious opposition in the congregation as long as the heat of the revival continued. However now that the religious atmosphere had cooled, his policy of church membership and communion became increasingly distasteful; and when he finally asked for permission to preach a series of sermons on the subject, he was flatly refused, and was therefore compelled to resort to writing. Under these circumstances, the reception which was accorded his *Humble Inquiry into the Qualifications for Communion* can easily be imagined. The four ministers who wrote a preface to it, knowing that it was a direct challenge, concluded their remarks with the following appeal to the congregation: "We heartily pray that the reverend author and his flock may for a long time be happy together; that their cordial love and tenderness to each other may continue and operate in mutual and all lawful condescensions and forbearances under different sentiments in these particulars; that everyone may be open to light, and guard against all prejudice, precipitance, and passion; that they may be very watchful against the devices of Satan to disunite or disaffect them; that they may study the things that make for

---

[16] Vol. IV, p. 432. *An Humble Inquiry into the Rules of the Word of God, concerning the Qualifications requisite to a Complete Standing and Full Communion in the Visible Christian Church* (1746).

peace and edification.—And the God of light, love and peace, will continue with them." [17]

It is possible that a compromise might have been reached, even on this fundamental issue, and Edwards might have been restored to the confidence of the congregation, had not another incident occurred previously, which had undermined Edwards' authority completely. I quote the story as told by Dr. Dwight in his *Life of Edwards*. "In the year 1744, Mr. Edwards was informed, that some young persons in the town, who were members of the church, had licentious books in their possession, which they employed to promote lascivious and obscene conversation, among the young people at home. Upon farther enquiry, a number of persons testified, that they had heard one and another of them, from time to time, talk obscenely; as what they were led to, by reading books of this gross character, which they had circulating among them. On the evidence thus presented to him, Mr. Edwards thought that the brethren of the church ought to look into the matter . . . The members of the church, with one consent and with much zeal, manifested it to be their opinion that it ought to be enquired into; and proceeded to choose a number of individuals as a Committee of Enquiry, to assist their pastor in examining into the affair. After this, Mr. Edwards appointed the time for the Committee of the church to meet at his house; and then read to the church a catalogue of the names

[17] Vol. IV, p. 288.

of the young persons, whom he desired to come to his house at the same time. . . .

"When the names were thus published, it appeared that there were but few of the considerable families in town, to which some of the persons named, either did not belong, or were not nearly related. . . . Before the day appointed for the meeting of the Committee arrived, a great number of heads of families altered their minds, and declared they did not think proper to proceed as they had begun, and that their children should not be called to an account in such a way for such conduct; and the town was suddenly all in a blaze. This strengthened the hands of the accused: some refused to appear; others, who did appear, behaved with a great degree of insolence, and contempt of the authority of the church: and little or nothing could be done further in the affair." [18]

This is but one instance, not only of the growing gulf between Mr. Edwards and his congregation, but also of the reaction, especially on the part of the younger generation, to the Great Awakening. From this time on, an influential group in the church began to desire his "separation." After many and protracted meetings of committees and councils, a resolution was finally adopted in 1749: "Whereas our Pastor, the Rev. Mr. Edwards, having separated and departed from the principles which the great Mr. Stoddard brought in and practised, and which he himself was settled upon, and a long time practised, with respect to the admission

[18] Vol. I, pp. 299-300. The biography of Edwards by Dwight, 1829.

of members in complete standing into the visible Church, whether it be not the opinion of the Church, that those principles are inconsistent with the principles of religion, and the peace of the Church and Town, and therefore desire a separation, he continuing in his principles." [19]

After another year of bickering he was not only dismissed from his church, but prohibited from preaching further in Northampton. Accordingly he and his family took their leave and, in January of 1751, he set out for the wilderness, having accepted the call of a handful of settlers in the frontier town of Stockbridge to become their minister, as well as the offers of the Society in London for Propagating the Gospel in New England and the Parts Adjacent to become a missionary to the Housatonic Indians. Broken and beaten, he was forced to abandon, not only Northampton and the churches and society of New England, but also the attempt to restore the Covenant of Grace, and all hope of the establishment of the Kingdom of God in New England. The last desperate attempt to erect it by an appeal to the affections had failed even more abruptly and decisively than had the political theocracy. The Great Awakening had proved to be but a dream.

Nevertheless Jonathan Edwards was not to be defeated. Though to all intents and purposes banished to the wilderness, he wasted little time in trying to establish the Kingdom of Heaven among the savages.

[19] Vol. I, p. 327. *Journal,* 1749.

He even wasted little time on the Stockbridge congregation. He regarded his supposedly strenuous mission field as an opportunity for solitude and leisure, and in this retirement he wrote his great philosophical works. In these he put before the world once more the idea of the sovereignty of God, and this time, not in the realm of church polity, not even in the wider realm of the religious affections, but in that eternal realm of philosophical speculation where the life of the imagination is free, where the exigencies of practical problems do not disturb the calm pursuit of distinct ideas, where the confusions of passion and the strife of parties can give place to the clarity of consistent thought and the finality of relentless dialectics. In this field Edwards was a master; the metaphysical system which he erected over the social ruins of the Holy Commonwealth established the Sovereignty of God on foundations which will outlast New England and all the churches of Christendom, for it is an expression of a philosophy which has always fascinated the human mind, and which seems to find a fresh but classic form in every age.

Jonathan Edwards had been from childhood of a speculative and scientific temper. When we remember the dominant moral and social interests of New England, this in itself is phenomenal. Perhaps this temper was due to the fact that political life was in his day less of an imaginative and intellectual enterprise, and more a mere matter of business and war; perhaps it is due to his extraordinary education; perhaps we must fall back, in the manner of the psychological sociologists, on his innate genius, or his introverted personality. All we know is that, being possessed of this scientific curiosity, he had the good fortune to go to Yale just at the time when Locke and Newton were being introduced. Instead of wading through the intricate verbiage of antiquated Puritan scholastics, as most of his contemporaries did, he started out with the most advanced science of his day. Physical science, of course, could not be expected to be his dominant interest, though his childhood observations on spiders are usually cited as evidence of an inductive and empirical interest in nature. The world in which he lived was not primarily the physical, and his experience was not primarily of nature. For us, looking back, it is fairly simple to distinguish what we call the empirical from what we call the supernatural elements in his philosophy, but to him and his contemporaries, this distinction would have been meaningless. The Puritans were empirically and actually pilgrims and strangers in this world; heaven really was their home; their whole sense of values and perspectives of imagination (realms of experience quite as basic as food, sex, sensation or knowledge) were dominated by their belief in the literal reality of the invisible world and by their consciousness of the all-pervading operations of God and the devil. Once human experience loses this quality, nothing can re-instate it. We feel as though we had at last awakened from a dream, or a night-mare, if you wish; what were vivid realities to them now fade into illusions, which, far from being elements of experience, are almost beyond our recall. For the Puritan, on the other hand, the situation was reversed. As he saw it, the incidents of our temporal sojourn are apt to lull us to sleep, and a petty preoccupation with fleeting goods and evils blinds us to the real issues of eternity. Hence the renewed sense of the Kingdom of God and of the eternal affairs of the soul was regarded as a great awakening. It is therefore natural that Jonathan Edwards should have been primarily interested in the science of this invisible world. All scientists, for that matter, are interested primarily in the invisible; they differ merely in their accounts of the nature of the forces operating underneath the visible flux.

To a Puritan the most natural science was the science of mind. Hence it need not surprise us that Edwards found Locke more fascinating than Newton, metaphysics more fascinating than physics, dialectics than experimentation. What may surprise us, however, is the overwhelming power which Locke's *Essay* had on this college sophomore, fourteen years of age. He found greater enjoyment in it, he tells us, "than the most greedy miser finds when gathering up handfuls of silver and gold, from some newly discovered treasure." In Locke's *Essay* he found a thoroughgoing attempt to make the mental world as intelligible as Newton had made the physical. It explained things which hitherto had been mysteries, and, what is more, it developed a method which might lead to still greater discoveries. Edwards immediately began to follow up its implications.[20] The scattered notes in which he develops these ideas are difficult to follow, but their general trend seems clear enough. He soon discovered that the general picture of the universe obtained by starting with Locke's "way of ideas" was quite identical with that obtained by starting with Newton's laws of motion.

There are two answers to the question, "In what do things exist?" Newton says, in absolute space; Locke, in the substance which underlies ideas. Now, starting with Locke, such ideas as color, taste and the secondary qualities, exist in the mind. Edwards proves, quite easily, that also the ideas of figure, motion, solidarity, extension, the "primary qualities" which Locke had relegated to some external substance, exist only in the mind. For all these primary ideas can be reduced to one, resistance, and the same arguments which Locke used to prove that color exists in the mind apply to resistance. Therefore nothing exists outside the mind. Therefore mind is the only substance. "That, which truly is the Substance of all Bodies, is the infinitely exact, and precise, and perfectly stable Idea, in God's

[20] The evidence that he knew the Cambridge Platonists and Norris's *The Ideal World* is circumstantial only, though the early Puritan ministers were, for the most part, bred at Cambridge and familiar with Platonism. The systems of William Ames and other Puritan scholastics, whom he knew, were full of Platonic notions, such as archetypes in the divine mind, etc. It has been proved beyond doubt that he could not have known of Berkeley's writings. It seems equally clear, in spite of a remark by Professor Riley to the contrary, that none of these Notes antedated his reading of Locke's *Essay*. For a discussion of the evidence, see Egbert C. Smyth: *Some Early Writings of Jonathan Edwards, A.D. 1714-1726*, in *American Antiquarian Society Proceedings*, New Series, Vol. X; and I. W. Riley: *American Philosophy: The Early Schools*, pp. 130-51.

mind, together with his stable Will, that the same shall gradually be communicated to us, and to other minds, according to certain fixed and exact established Methods and Laws." [21] "The world is therefore an ideal one; and the Law of creating, and the succession, of these ideas is constant and regular." [22]

Coming now to Newton's answer, absolute space, Edwards proves that all the physical properties of bodies are linked with motion. But a motionless universe, though it would contain no sensible objects, no resistance, no solidity, no measurable magnitudes and proportions, would still contain space. Space, therefore, is not a physical being; it is not on the same empirical basis as bodies in motion: "it is self-evident I believe to every man, that Space is necessary, eternal, infinite, and omnipresent. But I had as good speak plain: I have already said as much as, that Space is God." [23]

Both starting points lead to the same conclusion. All things, whether we call them bodies in motion or systems of related ideas, are concatenated into one great system, which, since it is in a measure intelligible to our finite minds, we may as well call the Divine Mind or God. "When we say that the World, i.e. the material Universe, exists no where but in the mind, we have got to such a degree of strictness and abstraction, that we must be exceedingly careful, that we do not confound and lose ourselves by misapprehension. That

[21] Vol. I, p. 674. *Notes on the Mind* (1717-1720).
[22] Vol. I, p. 669. *Notes on the Mind.*
[23] Vol. I, p. 706. *Notes on Natural Science.*

is impossible, that it should be meant, that all the world is contained in the narrow compass of a few inches of space, in little ideas in the place of the brain; for that would be a contradiction; for we are to remember that the human body, and the brain itself, exist only mentally, in the same sense that the other things do; and so that, which we call place, is an idea too. Therefore things are truly in those places; for what we mean, when we say so, is only, that this mode of our idea of place appertains to such an idea. We would not therefore be understood to deny, that things are where they seem to be. For the principles we lay down, if they are narrowly looked into, do not infer that. Nor will it be found, that they at all make void Natural Philosophy, or the science of the Causes or Reasons of corporeal changes; For to find out the reasons of things, in Natural Philosophy, is only to find out the proportion of God's acting. And the case is the same, as to such proportions, whether we suppose the World, only mental, in our sense, or no.

"Though we suppose, that the existence of the whole material Universe is absolutely dependent on Idea, yet we may speak in the old way, and as properly, and truly as ever. God, in the beginning, created such a certain number of Atoms, of such a determinate bulk and figure, which they yet maintain and always will, and gave them such a motion, of such a direction, and of such a degree of velocity; from whence arise all the Natural changes in the Universe, forever, in a continued series. . . . If a ball of lead were supposed to be let fall from the clouds, and no eye saw it, 'till it got within ten rods of the ground, and then its motion and celerity was perfectly discerned in its exact proportion; if it were not for the imperfection and slowness of our minds, the perfect idea of the rest of the motion would immediately, and of itself arise in the mind, as well as that which is there. So, were our thoughts comprehensive and perfect enough, our view of the present state of the world, would excite in us a perfect idea of all past changes.

"And we need not perplex our minds with a thousand questions and doubts that will seem to arise: as, To what purpose is this way of exciting ideas; and, What advantage is there in observing such a series. I answer, It is just all one, as to any benefit or advantage, any end that we can suppose was proposed by the Creator, as if the Material Universe were existent in the same manner as is vulgarly thought. For the corporeal world is to no advantage but to the spiritual; and it is exactly the same advantage this way as the other, for it is all one, as to any thing excited in the mind." [24]

"But," he immediately adds, "we have got so far beyond those things for which language was chiefly contrived, that, unless we use extreme caution, we cannot speak, except we speak exceeding unintelligibly, without literally contradicting ourselves." [25]

Whether it was because of these language difficulties,

[24] Vol. I, pp. 669-70. *Notes on the Mind.*
[25] Vol. I, p. 679. *Notes on the Mind.*

or because he saw it made no pragmatic difference
whether one used idealistic or Newtonian terminology,
or because he regarded his early speculations as trivial,
the fact remains, he did not return to them when he
resumed his philosophic writing during his exile in
Stockbridge. These school-boy compositions, on which
his philosophic fame is usually allowed to rest, were
practically discarded (though never denied) in his later
and maturer thought. The idealism which he now
developed,[26] though it did not retract these Lockian
and Newtonian ideas, was based on an entirely different set of categories; yet the outcome was essentially the
same. There is no evidence that he abandoned these
speculations out of fear of their possible consequences.
At no time does Edwards show intellectual fear, in spite
of the fact that he had been warned about the dangers
of Newton, Locke and the Deists. Nor did he show a
growing aversion to philosophy in favor of theology;
for he never had made such a distinction, and his later
writings, though, to be sure, more preoccupied with
traditional theological themes, were, for that very reason, not only in his own mind, but in that of his age,
more catholic and profound. Certainly they show no
signs of compromise in the interests of orthodoxy, nor
evidences of obtuseness to philosophical issues. There

---

[26] The greatest of these works is no doubt his *Inquiry into the Freedom
of the Will* (1754), though this is also his least original, being in large
part a development of the ideas in Locke's chapter on "Power" in the
Essay (1742). Of his other writings the most important and original are:
A Dissertation Concerning the Nature of True Virtue (1754); *A Dissertation Concerning the End for Which God Created the World* (1754); and
The Great Christian Doctrine of Original Sin Defended (1757).

is, of course, a curious contrast between that part of his writings which consists of rational argument and that which is largely Biblical commentary and theological polemics. But this was a characteristic of the intellectual heritage of his day, not a peculiar quality of his mind. The works of Hobbes, Locke, Leibnitz, and Newton, to mention only the greatest names, had this same trait. In addition to his belief in Biblical authority and theological tradition, Edwards employed rational inquiry thoroughly and fearlessly. He succeeded in reenforcing his faith, not by clinging to an antiquated science, nor by protesting against the growth of science, but by pushing to its logical conclusions the best science of his day.

Seemingly even before he had begun these college notes, based specifically on Locke and Newton, he had developed the idea of excellence in a way which, as far as we know, was quite original. And to this analysis of excellence, or beauty, he now returned. Here again we strike upon one of those amazing qualities of Edwards' thought. Esthetic categories are the last which one might expect to find in a rigid Calvinist philosophy, written in New England, by a Puritan of Puritans. Yet it is precisely on the theory of beauty, of harmony, of proportion, and of love, that Edwards now erected his imposing idealism. The only possible explanation is the fact that he had already conceived his religious experiences in these terms, and that he was now building his philosophy on those experiences. The extraordinary vividness of the language in which he describes excellence, love, and similar esthetic themes, leads us to the same conclusion; his philosophy in this its completest expression was essentially the product of his own experience, though formally it was but a new edition of Calvinism.

It is a commonplace that excellence, or beauty, consists in a certain equality or proportion among various elements. But why should proportion and equality be more beautiful than their opposites? Here we might be content with the empiricist's reply that this is simply an observed fact of human nature, but Edwards goes further. If beings are excellent or beautiful because some sort of agreement or proportion exists between them, this fact is a discovery about the nature of being in general. Being, in other words, is at its best when there is harmony among its parts. Obversely discord and disproportion are signs of imperfect being. They are the negative aspect of reality. Not that they do not exist, but that from the point of view of being itself, they are imperfections or blemishes. "That which is great has more existence, and is further from nothing, than that which is little. . . . An archangel must be supposed to have more existence, and to be every way further removed from non-entity than a worm." [27] Evil is not a positive entity, or force, in the world; it is merely the absence of order and beauty. A particular being, therefore, which has no relations, no *rapports,* or, to use Edwards' term, which does not consent to some other being, is not in the fullest sense

[27] Vol. III, p. 98. *On the Nature of True Virtue.*

a being at all. It has no excellence. In isolation it is lost, since its reality consists of the extent to which it finds itself consenting, not merely to other particular beings, but to that infinite harmony of parts which constitutes the nature of true beauty and the universal order of being. Strictly speaking, therefore, all being is one. This general being or harmony of existences we might as well term God, in whom we move and have our being, and there is none beside him. We exist literally in him. "God has infinitely the greatest share of existence. So that all other beings, even the whole universe, is as nothing in comparison of the divine Being." [28]

The bonds which unite the parts of being are not merely those of cause and effect. All things are, to be sure, caught up in an infinite system of cause and effect, but physical relations are, as it were, shadows of those proportions and harmonies which weld particular beings into a unity of excellence. Although the order of nature, on which the Deists and Newtonians are prone to dwell, is an evidence of God's glory, it is merely a small part of the ideal order of excellence which constitutes being. The natural philosopher, who sees only the beauty of nature and is blind to the greater beauties of the mind, has a very illiberal conception of God. The world of love and beauty is more than the natural world with its physical ties. Love is the primary bond

[28] Vol. III, p. 103. *A Dissertation Concerning the Nature of True Virtue* (1754, first published in 1765).

—love, first of all, toward God, and then, as if reflected, the love or consent of part toward part.

"As bodies, the objects of our external senses, are but shadows of beings; that harmony, wherein consists excellency and beauty, is but the shadow of excellency. That is, it is pleasant to the mind, because it is a shadow of love. When one thing sweetly harmonizes with another, as the Notes in musick, the notes are so conformed, and have such proportion one to another, that they seem to have respect one to another, as if they loved one another. So the beauty of figures and motions is, when one part has such consonant proportion with the rest, as represents a general agreeing and consenting together; which is very much the image of Love, in all the parts of a Society, united by a sweet consent and charity of heart." [29]

For the same reason that human excellence or virtue consists in the love of God, God's excellence must consist in his love of himself. Strictly speaking, God loves only himself, and he created the world with his own glory as his chief end. Obviously the happiness of human beings is not his end, for most human beings are lost. If a man seeks his own happiness apart from God, he merely displays his depravity; for, without the light of God in the soul, human life is lived in that outer darkness which encompasses brutes and devils. Ignoring God is the essence of sin and the source of damnation. Hence the only salvation for man is to

[29] Vol. I, p. 697. *Notes on the Mind*. This passage illustrates the fact that the esthetic categories were used even in his earliest writings.

consent to his sovereign, and to pray to be swallowed up in that divine excellence in which those to whom God gives the necessary grace may participate. "God and the creature, in the emanation of the divine fulness, are not properly set in opposition; or made the opposite parts of a disjunction. Nor ought God's glory and the creature's good, to be viewed as if they were properly and entirely distinct. . . . If we were capable of more perfect views of God and divine things, which are so much above us, it probably would appear very clear, that the matter is quite otherwise; and that these things, instead of appearing entirely distinct, are implied one in the other. God in seeking his glory, seeks the good of his creatures; because the emanation of his glory (which he seeks and delights in, as he delights in himself and his own eternal glory) implies the communicated excellency and happiness of his creatures. And in communicating his fulness for them, he does it for himself; because their good, which he seeks, is so much in union and communion with himself. God is their good. Their excellency and happiness is nothing but the emanation and expression of God's glory; God, in seeking their glory and happiness, seeks himself: and in seeking himself, i.e. himself diffused and expressed, (which he delights in, as he delights in his own beauty and fulness) he seeks their glory and happiness." [30]

What love God shows to his creatures is but a mode

[30] Vol. III, pp. 36-7. *A Dissertation Concerning the End for Which God Created the World* (1754).

of manifesting his glory, just as his wrath toward all who do not consent to him is equally a manifestation of his glory. The glory of God consists in the incarnation of beauty, and is therefore, both for God and for man, the only possible object of love. Man loves his fellow-man only in so far as he sees in him the reflection of the divine glory. There is, of course, a specious excellence in the instinctive order of physical bodies. The natural union and agreement which exists among animals, the symmetry in the features of the face, the harmony between the planets and their sun, these are instances of that secondary beauty which exists in nature blindly, as it were, since it is appreciated only when a being capable of the love of true excellence discovers in it the reflected image of God. Nature is not intrinsically perfect, but a rational mind, which loves perfection, finds that in nature, too, the glory of God is manifested. Unregenerate human nature is depraved, therefore, not in the sense that there is nothing of beauty in it, but in that it does not of its own power attain true virtue. All children of Adam are by nature fallible. Their instincts, without the guidance of the love of beauty, might accidentally produce an occasional excellence, but it would soon be ruined by an inevitable host of blunders. If they started life as fresh minds with a clean record, they might possibly be capable of that perfection which can face God without fear, but, starting as they do, as blind animals, freighted with an animal heritage traceable at least as far back as Adam, and with a social heritage no less irrational, they are all alike doomed to suffer the consequences of their common inheritance. Sin may be atoned for, but it can not be eradicated. Both sin and virtue, being relative to the whole system of being, and bearing endless consequences, are by nature infinite. They can not be measured quantitatively, nor does one balance the other. "An hour of adultery is not cancelled by a lifetime of loyalty"; it is to all eternity a blemish in being. This is the truth in that great Christian doctrine of original sin as Edwards defends it.

This is also the reason for that other great doctrine of divine sovereignty. Whether or not the saving love of God enters into a life is ultimately not a consequence of that individual's own choices and character. The vast majority of human beings are damned; that is, they never love true excellence, and this condition is not the result of their own free will, but of their station in the divine order. And if God is thus to be held responsible for the failures of life, what right have we to attribute the successes to ourselves? Indeed it is only by the grace of God that anybody is saved. No man's career is his own creation; for the whole system of being is involved in it. That saving love of excellence which now and then is seen in human beings is, therefore, a free and arbitrary gift of God; and its absence is likewise attributable to the sovereign will of God, who allows the great majority of men to suffer the natural fruits of their fallen state. Ultimately all deeds are acts of God. A man is but an actor playing the part which has been assigned to him. He can not miraculously escape the universal structure of the drama to which he belongs and act of himself, though in his romantic madness he may harbor such an illusion. All events involve the whole realm of being and are necessitated by it.

Rational beings, however, though they are under necessity, are not under the same sort of necessity which governs sticks and stones. Rational beings are subject to moral necessity, the necessity of making choices. God, by giving man a will, created a moral order, but the moral order is no less necessary than the physical. A man chooses, but how he chooses is absolutely determined by his understanding. The will is not a faculty or power which determines choices, it is but a name for the fact that man chooses. Being itself the determining factor, it can not be determined by itself. A choice is determined by "the apparent good as seen by the mind" at the moment, or, in other words, by "the last dictate of the understanding." A free will, being irresponsible, would lead to moral chaos. Only when the will is determined by the understanding is moral freedom possible, and only when the understanding is enlightened is it actual. But a human mind is, of course, itself a part of that necessary order which constitutes God's being, and God, inasmuch as he knows human minds, can foretell their choices. Nevertheless God's foreknowledge is not the cause of their choices; it is rather a consequence of the moral order. God, in creating the human mind, made man capable of the knowledge of good and evil, capable, that is, of judging by the same standards which govern God. God, therefore, can hold man responsible, not in the sense that man can control his own destiny, but in that he may know the moral quality of his actions and be governed by this knowledge. Not the capacity to perform, but the capacity to judge, is the basis of responsibility. God is perfectly just in condemning sinners, even though he knows they are unable to meet his requirements, for these sinners, however helpless, if they had the gift of reason, would condemn themselves.

The question naturally arises: Why did a perfectly excellent being create a world in which the majority of human beings will perish? Edwards replies: This miserable result is indeed the inevitable consequence of God's creating a moral order, but even a man, if confronted with the alternatives of a mechanical order, where everything would be automatically perfect, and a moral order, where human reason and will come into play, together with all the risks involved in it,— even a man would choose the moral order. Then how much more might we expect it of God! Man's tragic moral career is infinitely preferable to the dumb bliss of those animals or angels who know neither good nor evil. Mechanical perfection and moral judgment are the only alternatives rationally conceivable; and, since even God is subject to the necessary laws of reason, his choice of the moral order is an evidence of his excellence.

In this world, of course, human reason is very fallible; truth and error, good and evil, are jumbled together in hopeless confusion, and if this confusion were final the moral order would be a farce, not a tragedy. But the goal of the mind is clarity, and of the will, freedom. Eventually there must be a judgment day when confusion will be ended. At this last judgment the eyes of all will be opened to see the truth; each person will see himself as he really is. The wicked will then condemn themselves, and, asking to be treated according to their nature by being banished from the sight of God, will praise the glory of God manifested in their own banishment.

"Then shall the whole church be perfectly and for ever delivered from this present evil world; shall take their everlasting leave of this earth, where they have been strangers, and which has been for the most part a scene of trouble and sorrow: where the devil has reigned as God, and has greatly molested them, and which has been such a scene of wickedness and abomination; where Christ their Lord has been cruelly used; and where they have been so hated, reproached, and persecuted. They shall leave it, and shall never set foot on it again. And there shall be an everlasting separation made between them and wicked men. Before, they were mixed together, and it was impossible in many instances to determine their characters; but now all shall become visible; both saints and sinners shall appear in their true characters and forms. Then shall all the church be seen ascending to the right hand of Christ. . . .

"Christ, the glorious judge, shall pass that blessed sentence on the church at his right hand, Come ye blessed of my Father, inherit the kingdom prepared for you from the foundation of the world." [31]

In the very structure of being, God is seen to exhibit his sovereignty, and, in the philosophic heavens, the Holy Commonwealth exists eternally. Thus the social idealism which New England had rejected is sublimated and enshrined in the changeless structure of an idealistic metaphysics.

It is, of course, easy to dismiss all this as merely an ancient myth clothed in the language of philosophy. And it is easy to smile at the ever-present refuge which metaphysics affords to lost causes. It is even easier to shrug one's shoulders and condescendingly call what one fails to understand mysticism. But for one who is familiar with the language of the imagination, and who can see truths behind metaphors, this metaphysics must have more than a passing interest. All idealisms are metaphorical, or else mythological. They are at least cosmic projections of moral distinctions. Good and evil, confusion and clarity, sin and salvation, the state of nature and the state of grace, these are literally, of course, not beings but abstractions, not existences but distinctions. As distinctions, however, they are not arbitrary inventions of a superstitious soul, they are the familiar elements of the moral life. They are dialectically pure essences, distilled out of human experience.

[31] Vol. III, pp. 417, 419. *A History of the Work of Redemption* (1739, published in 1773 by his son).

To transform ideas into entities may be an unnecessarily laborious way of granting to the spirit a natural home, but it is, at least, less misleading than the effort to reconcile ideas and existences after having erected an infinite barrier between them. Dialectical distinctions, when transformed into metaphysical entities, may confuse the literally minded scientist, but they gain in reality for the person of imagination. They become actions and events in a cosmic drama. The life of the soul can then be projected into the very structure of being. This dramatization of the moral life is difficult, for the artist is continually under temptation to falsify the facts in the interests of the dramatic imagination. The figures in the drama are too easily treated with human sympathy, instead of with dialectical fidelity, each according to its nature. The traditional Christian drama of salvation has accordingly many versions, some profound, some sentimental; and when a somewhat original revision appears, like this of Edwards, the moralist is naturally interested in asking whether it has been made in the direction of presenting a more pleasing drama, or of preserving a greater fidelity to the underlying facts. Edwards' idealism undoubtedly does the latter, and this in spite of his own preoccupation with the literal meaning of the Christian myth. Everything is treated according to its nature; that is, the events and characters in the plot consistently embody stable ideas in their empirical functions. The drama is clearly a tragedy. The natural sordidness of life and the difficulty of attaining excellence and beauty are faced relentlessly. Human life is a confusion, and the final separation of good and evil is a goal, not an actuality. Sin is damned, not transcended. No man is master of his own destiny, nor responsible to himself alone. Only the love of pure beauty and of those beings in whom beauty is reflected makes life worth while. Beauty is its own end and justification. To it the wise man surrenders, whether he has enough grace to attain it or not, and the hope that it will some day be revealed without blemish or doubt sustains him.

Such is the general purport of the story, robbed of its metaphors. It is Puritanism purged of its local and mythological aspects and become an example of that catholic idealism which portrays in poetic language the nature of moral ideas, and which in all ages has found expression in one form or another.

As an idealist, Edwards will no doubt for some time to come be censured because he turned his back on the Lockian theory of knowledge and erected his system on a moral and esthetic basis quite independent of it. But already the supposedly necessary basis for idealism, which was developed by Locke, Berkeley, Hume and Kant, is rapidly falling into disrepute, and when these literal and academic systems with their numerous progenies lie buried, this more imaginative and metaphorical idealism, though probably not in Edwards' language, may yet return to mock its scientific rivals.[32]

---

[32] In fact, if we could finish our story, we should have occasion to witness its return even to New England in Josiah Royce's *The Problem of Christianity*.

As for Jonathan Edwards himself, he was a stumbling-block to his contemporaries, and a horrible example to his posterity. Whatever the value of his philosophy in its essential structure, the particular application he gave to it was even in his own day impractical, and today obviously absurd. Had his own love for God been less sentimental and pathological, had it resembled more the *amor intellectualis Dei* of Spinoza and of his own *Essay on the Freedom of the Will,* his philosophy would have exercised more power. As it was, however, his philosophical insight was buried under the ruins of his religion. He failed to see the futility of insisting on the Puritan principles. He preached humility to the proud. He tried to awaken a sense of sin in those who were becoming constantly more self-reliant. He defended the glory of God to those who were beginning to revel in their own glory. He believed in submission at a time when his countrymen were raising the cry of independence. He could not stem the current. In 1758 he accepted the presidency of Princeton, and died. And with his death, his ideas lost their vitality. We must, therefore, embark on those other mental and moral adventures which destroyed Puritanism and erected on its ruins a new world of the imagination, more secular, more free and more confused.

CHAPTER V

THE DISCOVERY OF ENGLAND

While Edwards in his frontier exile was rebuilding the metaphysics of Puritanism, the churches were groping for new and firmer foundations. After the dream of the Great Awakening, came the sober sense of disillusionment. When the excitement was over and weary minds were compelled to face the real world, they discovered that the old régime had disappeared. Not only were the old champions of the theocracy gone, but the whole world of ideas in which they had lived was strangely irrelevant. The utmost confusion reigned both in the churches and in the minds of the Puritans. Added to the innate anarchy of the congregational system was the fresh diversity produced by the enthusiasm. A large number of "separate" churches sprang up under the preaching of the New Light evangelists. These were forced to defend themselves both against the governments, which frequently tried to obstruct them, and against the learned divines, who felt nothing but scorn for this illiterate religion; they defended themselves by appealing to the new principles of natural rights and religious toleration. On the other side, the sober and conventional minds were forced to look for some adequate philosophy of "natural and reasonable" religion. For example, the Rev. Charles Chauncy, of the First Church, Boston, sounded the new note in his *Seasonable Thoughts on the State of Religion in New England* (1743); he shifted the whole basis of argument from Puritanism to liberalism, from the idea of salvation to the idea of reason. Others, instead of reacting in the direction of English rationalism, sought refuge in the order and dignity of the Church of England and urged the need of bishops to bring order out of chaos. At this suggestion the liberals flew into a rage: one more controversy had started. Thus the stage was set for a variety of religious and philosophical conflicts, to most of which the old Puritanism was quite irrelevant. These new conflicts found their intellectual weapons, not in the New England tradition, but in the contemporary philosophies of Old England. New philosophies, of which the Puritans had been ignorant, were freshly imported from England and served the intellectual needs of a new generation. The wars of the Lord against the unregenerate made way for the party struggles between English Tories and Whigs, Anglicans and Liberals. As far as the clergy were concerned, the American Revolution had begun.[1] The effect of these events on the philosophy of Puritanism is amply illustrated in the lives of Samuel Johnson, who discovered the Church of England, and Jonathan Mayhew, who discovered the Deism of the English liberals. In both cases the story takes

[1] See Alice M. Baldwin: *The New England Clergy and the American Revolution* (Duke Univ. Press, 1928).

us to college libraries, where young men, after they had read the assignments in the Puritan classics required by their innocent old tutors, discovered a totally different learning in the best English authors of the day.

Samuel Johnson, the son of a deacon, was born in 1696 at Guilford, Connecticut. What little schooling he could acquire in this pioneer community was given him by his grandfather and by the ministers of the neighboring towns, several of whom were, even in the eyes of this ten-year-old lad "such wretched poor scholars that they could teach him little or nothing." [2]

"The condition of learning (as well as everything else) was very low in these times indeed much lower than in the earlier time while those yet lived who had had their education in England and first settled the country. These were now gone off the stage and their sons fell greatly short of their acquirements as through the necessity of the times they could give but little attention to the business of education. . . . It was nothing but the scholastic cobwebs of a few little English and Dutch systems that would hardly now be taken up in the street, some of Ramus and Alstad's Works was considered as the highest attainments. They heard indeed, in 1714, when he took his Bachelor's Degree, of a new philosophy that of late was all in vogue and of such names as Descartes, Boyle, Locke, and Newton,

[2] Herbert and Carol Schneider (Editors): *Samuel Johnson, President of King's College, His Career and Writings* (New York, 1929), Vol. I, p. 4. (*Memoirs of the Life of the Rev. Dr. Johnson.*) Subsequent citations refer to this edition of Johnson's works.

but they were cautioned against thinking anything of them because the new philosophy it was said would soon bring in a new divinity and corrupt the pure religion of the country, and they were not allowed to vary an ace in their thoughts from Dr. Ames' *Medulla Theologiæ* and *Cases of Conscience* and Wollebius, which were the only systems of divinity that were thumbed in those days and considered with equal if not greater veneration than the Bible itself for the contrivance of those and the like scholastical authors to make curious systems in a scientific way out of their own heads, and under each head to pick up a few texts of Scripture which seemed to sound favorably and accommodate them to their preconceived schemes.

"Indeed there was no such thing as any book of learning to be had in those times under a 100 or 150 years old, such as the first settlers of the country brought with them 70 or 80 years before and some few used to make synopses or abridgements of these old scholastic systems." [3]

Several of Samuel Johnson's college note-books have survived. They give a startling picture of the intellectual horizons and educational methods in the college, which was then being established, and which later bore the name of Yale. In a little volume, written in what was supposed to be Latin, and dedicated to "dignissimo, clarissimo, doctissimo, spectatissimo viro Magistro Phinea Fisk," he made a systematic summary of all learning. It is entitled *Technologia sive Technometria;*

[3] Vol. I, pp. 5-6. *Memoirs.*

Ars Encyclopaidia manualis ceu philosophia. Editio quarto longe correctior. Anno a Christo pro nobis incarnato 1714 et a mundo per numen creato 5663.[4] It consists of about twelve hundred theses, each containing a definition or a classification. The whole work is an imposing scheme of classification. Art (the *Summum genus*) is divided according to species and according to genera. The species into archetypes and types. The types into entypes and ectypes. Ectypes into rules, methods and species. Species as follows:

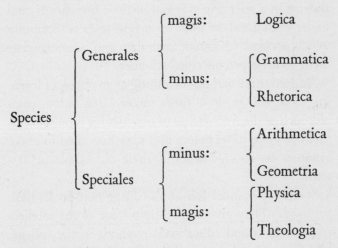

Species	Generales	magis:	Logica
		minus:	Grammatica / Rhetorica
	Speciales	minus:	Arithmetica / Geometria
		magis:	Physica / Theologia

Each of these arts is then subdivided almost *ad infinitum*. A few examples from the *Physica* will suffice to illustrate the quality of this encyclopedic learning:

"874. The inanimate mixtures are without soul.
"875. And are either meteorological or geological.

[4] Vol. II, pp. 55-186.

"876. Meteorological is an inanimate object of imperfect mixture and therefore suddenly comes and as suddenly goes.

"885. A geological phenomenon is an inanimate and more perfect mixture of sulphur and quick-silver.

"886. It has principles and species.

"887. Its principles are sulphur and quick-silver.

"888. Sulphur is the hotter and drier principle.

"889. Quick-silver is the moister and colder principle.

. . . .

"944. So far the body. The sensitive soul is the elemental spirit which is the principle of sensation, appetite and motion.

"945. Its faculties are therefore these three.

"946. Sense is the faculty of the sensitive soul by which the animal senses single objects.

"947. Sensation requires an organ, an object and a congruous medium.

"948. Senses are external or internal.

. . . .

"959. The internal sense is one by which an animal perceives internally the objects perceived externally and judges them.

"960. Its acts are imagination, thought and memory.

. . . .

"995. Man is a rational animal or one whose principal soul is the rational soul.

"996. His properties are speech, or his system of mental symbols by articulate sound; his ability to laugh, or his sign of joy; weeping, or his sign of grief.

"997. All animals both man and beast are male or female by nature stronger or weaker.
"998. All these natural beings orderly assembled in a round whole is *the world*.
"999. The world is the ordered structure of all natural beings dependent on one principle and tending to one end." [5]

Now let us return to Johnson's autobiography: "Mr. Johnson was thought to excel at this [making synopses] having drawn up a little system of all parts of learning then known in nothing else but a curious cobweb of distributions and definitions which only served to blow him up with a great conceit that he was now an adept, and in this pleasing imagination he continued a year or two, till accidentally lighting on Lord Bacon's *Instauratio Magna, or Advancement of Learning* (perhaps the only copy in the country and nobody knew its value), he immediately bought it and fell to studying it.

"About this time, 1714, when he was turned of 18, came over from England a well chosen library of new books collected by Mr. Dummer, agent for the Colony. He had then all at once the vast pleasure of reading the works of our best English poets, philosophers, and divines, Shakespeare and Milton, etc., and Norris, etc., Boyle and Newton, etc., Patrick and Whitby, Barrow, Tillotson, South, Sharp, Scot and Sherlock, etc. All this was like a flood of day to his low state of mind." [6]

The effect was truly revolutionary. His next note-

[5] Vol. II, pp. 145-56, *passim*.　　[6] Vol. I, pp. 6-7. *Memoirs*.

book, which served to guide his teaching at the college
as well as his further studies, is a remarkable contrast.
It is written in English, and though still in the form of
an encyclopedia of learning, it is preoccupied, not with
formal distinctions, but with new subject-matter.
Bacon's influence on him was primarily to shake him
loose from his scholasticism and conceit. Bacon
kindled his imagination and gave him a glimpse of
the enormous reaches of human ignorance and the
possibilities of the advancement of learning.[7] The following subtitle of his new encyclopedia [8] is certainly
Baconian in spirit: "These are the System of Travails
of the Human Intellect in the Microcosm and in the
Macrocosm." The content, however, of his philosophy
was largely derived, not from Bacon, but from Locke
and his contemporaries. His new classification of the
sciences suggests that of Locke at the end of his *Essay*,
and both the *Logic* and the new *Introduction to Philosophy* are conceived in Lockian terms. Formal logic
is almost entirely abandoned and his attention is centered on the problems of guiding the process of thinking and improving its quality. As for Newton and
natural philosophy, Johnson soon discovered that he
needed calculus to understand it at all. Accordingly he

[7] In his note-book at a later date he inserted the following: "When I
was at College I was taught nothing but to be a conceited coxcomb like
those that taught me. Indeed we had no books and our ignorance made
us think almost out of our own brains as a certain Gent. (Mr. Noyes) of
those times used to say was his way." Vol. II, p. 57.

[8] *Some General Speculations Being an Introduction Unto Sophia, or
Philosophy, by Samuel Johnson, A.B., Guilford, May and June, Anno
Domini 1716.* See Vol. II, pp. 201-16.

studied higher mathematics by himself and learned the rudiments of modern physics and astronomy.

All this took place in the few years he remained at Yale as tutor. He immediately introduced the new learning into the curriculum, and it may have been through him that his pupil, Jonathan Edwards, came in contact with Locke. Johnson even began to talk about natural religion and enjoyed reading the milder Deists, such as Boyle and Wollaston. In the meantime there was continual trouble at the college. Financial difficulties, local jealousies, and several other factors, disrupted the school. One of these factors was Johnson himself. The students complained that he was too poor a scholar to teach them; he was so unpopular, whatever the real reason may have been, that he was practically forced to resign in 1720. He became the pastor of a small congregation at West Haven, near enough to the school so that he could continue his studies.

During these years he not only discovered the new learning but also the Anglican Church, for among the books in the library sent over in 1714 by Dummer, Governor Yale's agent, were many by Anglican divines. In these writers he found a rich and scholarly tradition of which he had been quite ignorant. And, most important of all to his own mind, he was made conscious by these ecclesiastics of the doubtful validity of his Congregational ordination. Then, too, he learned something of the wealth of secular poetry and literature which England had produced during the seventeenth

century, of which he had hitherto not the faintest notion. In short, Johnson made the discovery that New
England was really not the center of God's Kingdom
on earth, but rather merely one of the outlying prov-
inces of the British Empire. He was shocked at the
intellectual backwardness of his colony; he was disgusted with the controversial temper and lack of order
among the Congregational churches. On all sides
he seemed to see evidences of provincialism, intellectual
poverty, and in general a lack of civilization. In 1722
he and a few friends, after years of hesitation and de-
liberation, finally resolved to cross the Atlantic and
take Orders in the Anglican Church. When Johnson,
arriving in England, discovered the glories of London,
the learning of Oxford, and the dignity of the episcopal
hierarchy; when, in other words, he became sensible of
the values of civilization or what in New England was
known as worldliness; his Puritan prejudices quickly
subsided. He became an Englishman and a gentleman.
From that time on he looked upon America as a mis-
sion-field; not, of course, in the crude way in which the
Society for the Propagation of the Gospel in Foreign
Parts, whose missionary he now became, looked at it,
not as a land of heathen natives, but as a frontier
settlement, crude, uncouth, ungoverned, dependent for
salvation upon a mother-country and her mature institutions.

To read his own account of this crisis gives one the
impression that the real issue at stake was whether or
not the Christians of the "purest age," the first century,

had bishops. For years this question was argued back and forth by him and his friends, before they finally decided to break with the Congregational system, and for years they read church histories, sermons and debates on the primitive and true form of church government. But to mistake the theoretical form and technical questions of this debate for its real motives would be as trivial as to mistake the propaganda of the War for a discussion of its causes. It is quite easy to read between the lines of Johnson's account what was actually going on in his mind, and occasionally he is explicit, conscious that a whole philosophy is involved. He tells us, for example, in his diary, among the reasons for his decision: "This country is in such a miserable state as to church government (let whatever hypothesis will, be right) that it needs reformation and alteration in that affair. . . . There may be more souls damnified for want of episcopal government in the country and that by far at length, than by making this appearance." [9] And just before he set sail from Boston for England, he entered the following in his journal: "This day, by God's grace I first communicated with the Church of England. How devout, grand, and venerable was every part of the administration, every way becoming so awful a mystery!" [10]

In his autobiography he tells us: "Though Mr. Johnson was always of a serious devout turn of mind, yet he never liked enthusiasm, which then obtained much

[9] Vol. I, pp. 63-4. *Liber Dierum Samuel Johnsonis, 1722-31.*
[10] In E. E. Beardsley: *Life and Correspondence of Samuel Johnson, D.D.* (New York, 1873), p. 23.

in the country. . . . What first prejudiced him against this was his observation, when at College of its great tendency to promote and nourish self-conceit and spiritual pride. The scholars had private meetings for prayer and reading and such as had something of a knack that way could not forbear appearing vain of it; one especially who excelled at it was even so vain as to talk of his gifts; on the other hand some modest youths of good sense who wanted assurances to pray off-hand at any rate, were apt to be despised and discouraged. He also often observed many impertinent and indecent and sometimes almost blasphemous expressions dropt, which were very shocking to him, which gave him early disgust and led him to think surely it must be much better that our prayers be precomposed in the best manner possible."

"What chiefly contributed to a very great increase of the Church [of England] was a strange, wild enthusiasm that was propagated through the country by means of Mr. Whitefield's preaching about in all parts of it, with the high approbation and applause of the dissenting ministers, who thought this would most effectually confound the Church, as he was a minister of the Church, and yet preached in their way and inculcated many Calvinistical notions. In consequence of this, many of them broke through all order and rule as he had done, and strolled about from place to place and these were soon followed with a numerous fry of lay exhorters, propagating the most horrid notions both of God and the Gospel that could enter into the heart of man. The way of these teachers and exhorters was, in the most affecting tones to say all the most frightful things they could think of about the devil, hell, and damnation, so as to scare people almost out of their wits, in order to bring them to what they called conversion; several went quite distracted, so that their night meetings (in several of which Mr. Johnson was present *incog.*) looked like a very hell upon earth; some sighing, some groaning, some screeching and wringing their hands, the minister all the while, like a fiend tormenting them, till they would come to Christ; while others who conceited they were converted, were all in the greatest raptures, and transports, triumphing and singing psalms and hallelujahs and some fell into trances and saw Christ and angels, and who were saved, and who were damned; and others censuring and calling all to nought for the vilest Pharisees and hypocrites those who were not converted in their way, pretending they could see hell and the devil in their faces, etc., etc. Such hideous doings as these threw the country into the greatest confusion imaginable and occasioned endless divisions and separations, so that many could find no rest to the sole of their feet till they retired into the Church as their only ark of safety. Thus what they expected would be the ruin of the Church proved the greatest means of its increase and enlargement."

"He had likewise been always much embarrassed with the rigid Calvinistical notions in which he had been bred. He thought that he must believe them because everybody else did and because some sounds in

Scripture seemed to favor them. . . . When therefore the Library came, and he and his friends above mentioned came to read and consider these excellent divines of the Church, especially Scot and Whitby, and conversed together on these subjects, it was with vast satisfaction that they saw infinite reason to make their minds easy about them. However the times were such that they found it necessary to be very cautious and keep their thoughts to themselves. He had also an early dislike to the independent or congregational form of church government, in which every brother has a hand; which as well as the *extempore* way he plainly saw tended too much to conceit and self-sufficiency and to endless feuds, censoriousness and uncharitableness while the discipline was often on mere human frailties and made a means to revenge little private quarrels and issued in great animosities and often in virulent separations. He was convinced that a way so entirely popular could but very poorly and he thought not long subsist, to answer any ends of government; but must from the nature of it crumble to pieces, as every individual seemed to think himself infallible." [11]

To Benjamin Franklin he wrote: "Would to God you were charged with pleading the same cause in behalf of all the Governments that they might all alike be taken into the King's more immediate protection. It would certainly be best for us all to be under one form of government, and I beg that your best influence may be so directed, that the Government at home

[11] Vol. I, pp. 10-11, 28, 11-12. *Memoirs.*

when they take yours in hand may make but one work of it. I wish to Heaven, particularly in behalf of this, that that might be the happy event, for we greatly suffer for want of such a change, particularly by our whole Assembly's being the judges in all cases of equity, and our Constitution's being so monstrously popular that all our judges and other officers depend entirely on the people, so that they are under the strongest temptation in many cases to consider not so much what is law or equity, as what may please their constituents." [12]

And to the Archbishop of Canterbury he complained about "such loose thinkers as Mayhew, who can scarcely be accounted better Christians than the Turks, or such furious bitter Calvinistical enthusiasts as are really no more friends to monarchy than episcopacy; and against people of both these sorts episcopacy is really necessary towards the better securing our dependence, as well as many other good political purposes." [13]

These and many similar passages in his writings make it quite evident that Samuel Johnson was thoroughly disillusioned about the whole Puritan philosophy, its spiritual pride, its indecent enthusiasm, its Calvinism, its democracy and anarchy. In the Church he found an ark of refuge; he found learning, law and order, "the beauty of holiness," urbanity. He returned to a civilized world, upon which the Puritans had turned their backs in favor of their own Holy Com-

[12] Vol. I, p. 349. Undated letter, probably 1765.
[13] Vol. I, p. 346. Sept. 20, 1764.

monwealth, but to which they themselves were inevitably, though clandestinely, returning. He had recovered a worldly sense of values, for he was willing to judge religion by its moral fruits, rather than to sacrifice morality to an unearthly ideal. His sense of sin had been transformed into a sense of ignorance, and his Yankee pride into a genuine piety.

Johnson had aimed to settle down to the peaceful life of a small parish, there to devote himself to his simple duties and above all to his favorite studies, but by the irony of fate he was doomed to add one more controversy to the long list of religious disputes which were harassing New England, and from which he himself had desired to escape. A public *Letter to His Dissenting Parishioners* in defense of the Anglican Church naturally called for replies, and these for rejoinders. And in the '40's, as a result of the Great Awakening and its emphasis on "mere sovereignty" and special grace, he was led into a protracted dispute with several Calvinists on this fundamental theological issue. He protested profusely that he disliked debate and adopted a very conciliatory and dignified manner, but this merely piqued his more frankly contentious antagonists. Jonathan Dickinson, one of the most violent of his Calvinist adversaries, died in the midst of the dispute, on which occasion Samuel Johnson remarked: " 'Methinks a man must be not a little out of countenance to find himself in this (disputatious) temper translated into the calm and peaceable regions of the blessed.' I could' wish he might have had opportunity to cool after so great a part of his life spent in wrangling against the Church in one shape or other, and that, as far as I could ever see, without any just argument or fair reasoning." [14] This bit of sarcasm was strong language for Johnson, but it was nothing compared with the abuse and *ad hominem* tactics of his opponents. Johnson probably had the better of the argument, but he had no opponent like Jonathan Edwards, for whom he would hardly have been a match. Johnson, in fact, insisted on several of the distinctions which Edwards was at that very time developing into his *Essay on the Will.* He admitted that God was not responsible for everything he foreknew (or, strictly speaking, *knew,* since in God time is transcended); and he admitted that "in the distribution of talents and favors in this state of probation, the sovereignty of God as a benefactor does truly take place; but" (and here we come to the heart of the question) "in the future distributions of rewards and punishments, absolute sovereignty is entirely out of the question. As a judge deciding the eternal condition of men, God never once represents himself as arbitrary, but everywhere, as proceeding according to equity, without respect of persons; not treating men according to any absolute disposition he hath already made, but in exact proportion to their own conduct in the use of the talents com-

[14] In Johnson's Preface to *A Second Vindication of God's Sovereign Free Grace Indeed,* by John Beach, 1748. See Vol. III, p. 206. Johnson quotes the first sentence from Archbishop Tillotson.

mitted to their trust." [15]   Now the *use* to which a man puts his talents and his circumstances, he argued, is a matter of his free will and is not necessitated by a particular decree either of God or of fate.   To God, of course, all things are neither necessary nor contingent, they are *certain* and known, but to us there is a difference between necessary and contingent events. "Events are then said to be necessary, as to us, when they derive from the settled course of nature, the laws of which are established by the free will, and invariably executed by the almighty power of God, having no dependence on our will, nor have we, at all any power over them, though they are mere arbitrary constitutions of the will of God conformable to the dictates of his infinite wisdom, and therefore can be known to him only as being his own establishments.   Such are, the descent of heavy bodies to the earth; the revolutions of the sun, moon and stars, and the return of the seasons and tides; the course of vegetation and sensation, and the condition and abilities of each individual, etc.   But by contingent events, we mean such as depend on our own free wills and self-exertions; as that I am now writing, when I might, if I pleased, have been visiting a neighbor. These things, being fact, are as certain, and as certainly known, as the other; but it by no means follows that they are therefore necessary; nor can they be, because they immediately depend on our free wills (who are intuitively conscious of our free agency) and not on the

[15] Vol. III, p. 176.   *A Letter Concerning the Sovereignty and the Promises of God* (1745).

will of God (any otherwise than as our existence depends on his will) who therefore does not know them because he wills them; but he therefore knows them because they are, by his intuitive knowledge, to which all things, at once are present, in a manner, indeed, which we can have no notion of, though we can demonstrate that it must be so. These things therefore are contingent as depending on the liberty of free agents, and when future are uncertain with respect to us, though they are certain with respect to God." [16]

Johnson's assumption that we have an intuitive knowledge of our freedom was naturally questioned, for he was arguing in the presence of those victims of the evangelists who actually felt the lack of freedom, and some of whom even had a horrible premonition of their predetermined damnation. In this predicament Johnson fell back on a pragmatic device which reminds one of William James' tactics on essentially the same problem. He argued that "the right way of forming a just notion of God's decrees, is to judge of them by the facts before our eyes. If, therefore, it be a fact, that by the disposition which God hath already made, or by any necessitating influence of his on the one hand, or withholding it on the other, to each individual, the good are necessarily good and happy, and the bad are necessarily bad and miserable, God doubtless absolutely decreed it should be so." [17] Fol-

[16] Vol. III, p. 189. *Letter to Mr. Jonathan Dickinson, in Defense of Aristocles to Authades, Concerning the Sovereignty and Promises of God* (1747).
[17] Vol. III, p. 199. *Ibid.*

lowing this clue, Johnson soon discovered that, as a question of fact, this was unanswerable, for no one can either prove or disprove that a man must be what he is. Empirically all we know is that regeneration takes place by degrees. Men are more or less saved. "Is there no medium between an obstinate relentless sinner, and one that is thoroughly regenerate, in your sense of the word, *i.e.,* that has gained the mastery of his lusts, and is universally in heart and life devoted to God in Jesus Christ? May not one who is not yet thus entirely devoted to God, be brought by the assistance of common grace, . . . to be serious and really solicitous for salvation, so as being deeply sensible of his own guilt and weakness, earnestly to cry to God for help and to strive in earnest that he may be qualified for God's help?" [18]

In this way Johnson tried to escape the dilemma which the Calvinists had proposed to him. They had argued that God's promises were merely "encouragements," but that, strictly speaking, they were superfluous, for he could not make promises to the unregenerate since they wholly lacked redeeming grace, and he would not make promises to the regenerate since they already possessed it. Johnson, by conceiving of regeneration as a process, not a fixed state, found room for an encouraging, though not for an invincible, grace. God promises to help those who are doing their own best. But speaking of salvation in these terms

[18] Vol. III, pp. 179-80. *A Letter Concerning the Sovereignty and Promises of God* (1745).

was equivalent to regarding its outward moral mani-
festations as its very essence; and no doubt Johnson
came dangerously near upsetting the whole philosophy
of grace, just as the Calvinists came dangerously near
upsetting the philosophy of promises. In reality, however, this was precisely Johnson's aim, though he
would not admit it in any radical form. He regarded
the doctrine of invincible grace as demoralizing, and in
order to give due weight to human responsibility for
moral conduct, he fell back on man's free will or
absolute agency. The distinction between physical and
moral necessity, which Edwards made fundamental,
Johnson regarded as irrelevant. It is true, he admitted,
that a man is morally forced to "assent to self-evident
truth" just as he is physically exposed to the force of
gravity, but though man is passive in the face of both
truth and gravity, he is nevertheless free in his realm of
will and action. "Be my mind ever so much necessitated to assent to evident truth, I am nevertheless free
to choose or refuse, to act or not to act, in consequence
of this assent; for action according to the frame of
our nature, ever springs from a self-asserting power." [19]

"I must think there can scarcely be a more mis-
chievous doctrine advanced among mankind than this
necessitating doctrine of yours; for it tends at once to
destroy all religion and morality, and all civil and family government, and render them unmeaning and
ridiculous things; for what signify all laws and rules of

[19] Vol. III, p. 209. Preface to *A Second Vindication of God's Sovereign
Free Grace Indeed* (1748).

action, all motives taken from praise or blame, hope or fear, reward or punishment, while every thing we do is under a fatal necessity, and we can do no otherwise than we do. Let a child, a servant, or a subject be but possessed with this principle, that he can do no otherwise than he does, and in vain do you attempt to persuade him to do better, and it must be the greatest injustice to punish him for doing worse." [20] With this *ad hominem* appeal he closes his argument, and though it is dialectically feeble, it at least represents the underlying moral motives which repelled him from the Calvinist doctrine, and in view of the hysterical and fanatical consequences of the doctrine in the hands of the evangelists, he felt himself empirically quite justified, whatever his dialectic may have proved or failed to prove.

It was for similar reasons that he welcomed Berkeley's idealism. In his early enlightenment, it may be remembered, Johnson was very receptive to the ideas of Locke, Newton, and the milder Deists. The admirable harmony and laws of nature which they emphasized delighted him as being reason's witness to God. It never occurred to him that there was the least conflict between the latest science of nature and the oldest truths of revelation. But Dean Berkeley, who spent two and a half years in Rhode Island, and whom Johnson naturally visited because of their close ecclesiastical affiliation, began to tell him of the direction in

[20] Vol. III, p. 200. *Ibid.*

which Newton's philosophy was leading, of how Collins, starting from the Deistic position, had proved the doctrine of fate and the impossibility of the existence of God; and Samuel Johnson, himself, discovered the deterministic implications of Locke and the tendency toward free-thinking in Wollaston, Shaftesbury and others. He then became alarmed and gave a ready ear to Berkeley's attack on Newton.

Berkeley's wholesale attack on matter worried Johnson at first, but when he discovered that Newton's laws of motion, and the physical sciences in general, were as valid as ever, that Berkeley was merely removing the mechanical substances of matter and space, together with all mechanical or secondary causes, and that spirits were proved to be the only operating agents, Johnson was delighted with the philosophy.

What he emphasized first of all was that resistance, a quality which Newton had attributed to the operation of the *vis inertiæ* of matter, was here proved to be a direct operation of God upon the mind of man. Strictly speaking (and he insisted vigorously on this point in his correspondence with Cadwallader Colden), inertia is no *vis,* or power, at all. Matter *is* inertia, purely passive; it must be moved by something extraneous to it. In this sense, matter was pragmatically identical with the ideas in the divine mind, which exist external to our own minds, but which have no power. They imply as their necessary correlative an active principle, mind, will or spirit.

This spirit is more than a name for the act of perceiving. For, in the act of perceiving, a human mind is really passive; it merely receives what God, the active mind, impresses upon it. Likewise in intuiting self-evident truths, which must also come from God, though not by the external senses, a human mind is literally compelled to see the truth. Berkeley's emphasis on *percipere* as the *esse* of a spirit, worried Johnson not a little; for, in that case, what happens when the mind ceases perceiving? How can it be immortal? Does it coalesce with the divine mind, just as when we fall asleep our ideas have an external and stable existence in the divine mind? If so, what becomes of human freedom? We have escaped physical fatalism merely to fall into the clutches of Calvinistic determinism. Berkeley accordingly admitted, and Johnson emphasized, the ultimate and indefeasible existence of finite minds as free active powers, in essence as free as God, though in practice limited by God's willingness to communicate himself both in nature and in thought. Each person is therefore responsible for his acts, and God, only for his ideas. God furnishes us inert material or subject-matter, but the use we put it to is in an absolute sense our own. This emphasis on free-will was developed by Johnson primarily to combat the Calvinists, and it is important to note that the idealism represented by Johnson and Berkeley was erected in direct opposition to that of Edwards. Edwards' was monistic and deterministic; Berkeley's was pluralistic and "Arminian." This pluralistic idealism served two purposes: it gave a new philosophic basis for human freedom, thus undermining the Puritan idealism of Edwards; and it made a bold attack on the new determinism of Newtonian science. Edwards had made his peace with Newton, but Berkeley upset the whole framework of natural science and brought philosophy back much closer to the principles of revelation. Berkeley transformed nature into a constant succession of miraculous revelations of God to man.

Though this idealism had much eased Johnson's mind, he was still philosophically nervous. For even in Berkeley's philosophy it was a far cry from the discoveries of reason to the doctrine of the Trinity, the belief in angels, and similar mysteries of the Christian tradition. Johnson was therefore overjoyed when he discovered that a certain Thomas Hutchinson in England had proved the scientific value of the Bible. He announced his discovery as follows: "It is remarkable that Bishop Berkeley in Ireland, Mr. Hutchinson in England, and Abbé Pluche in France, the greatest men of the age, without any communication with each other should at the same time, though by different media come into the same conclusion, namely, that the Holy Scriptures teach the only true system of natural philosophy as well as the only true religion, and that Mr. Franklin in America should at the same time without any design, by his electrical experiments greatly confirm it." [21]

[21] Vol. I, p. 45. *Memoirs.* "Mr. Hutchinson appeared to him to be a prodigious genius, little inferior if not superior to Sir Isaac himself, and to have even very much unhinged his (Sir Isaac's) main principles and proved his inconsistency; and to have established the only right

Johnson now became obsessed with the study of Hebrew. He made it a basic part of the curriculum of King's College; he preached sermons re-interpreting Hebrew texts; he taught Hebrew to his six-year-old grandson; and he devoted the last years of his life to writing a Hebrew Grammar. This misplaced scientific enthusiasm is more than amusing, it is pathetic; for it is a tribute to a mind which would not compromise, and which followed fearlessly a doomed philosophy. His dominant purpose, which he himself said was "to make the study of nature subservient to religion," was profoundly conceived. He scorned the popular idea that science is science and religion is religion, and each must tolerate the other. Such a separation of powers was as much a confession of fear of knowledge as the political doctrine of checks and balances is a confession of fear of government. A genuine devotee of wisdom will never stop until he has made the study of nature

system of philosophy from the Bible; and as to his divinity it appeared (1) That there was the highest probability that he had discovered some very important ancient truths that had been in a manner lost, particularly with regard to the divine names, the Cherubim, etc. (2) That he had, in the most effectual manner confuted both the Jews, infidels, and Arians and other erroneous Christians. (3) That by explaining the ancient language and hieroglyphics, he had made it very evident that the whole method of our redemption by Christ was much more clearly explained by God, and understood by our first parents both by the patriarchal and Mosaic ages, than has been commonly imagined. (4) That as he had shown the origin of philosophy and religion, so he had given the best account of the origin of idolatry, that is anywhere to be met with. In a word though in many things he seemed to overdo and go into extremes and his language was obscure, yet, no man in these last ages, ever appeared to have so laboriously studied and so thoroughly understood the Hebrew language and antiquities as Mr. Hutchinson." "Mr. Hutchinson's Scripture philosophy shows plainly by many passages from the ancients that this was indeed the original and most ancient system." Vol. I, pp. 30-1, 45. *Memoirs.*

subservient to religion, or, to put it into less offensive language, to make religion grow out of a scientific understanding of nature. In this he possessed neither the dialectical skill nor the imagination of Berkeley and Edwards, but he was more persistent than either of them in re-uniting two realms of the mind which were constantly diverging. He had an implicit faith in the scientific value of the orthodox theology, and his enormous efforts to prove this true made him appear grotesque even to his contemporaries, but at least he revealed thereby a greater intellectual sincerity and a profounder sense of the issues ultimately at stake. Both Berkeley and he had the misfortune to seize upon an obsolescent tradition to help them out of the difficulties they found in a new one.

Johnson was no less unfortunate than Berkeley in being forced to witness how infidels exploited his clever dialectics for their own sinister ends. Johnson's espousal of Berkeley's idealism, to be sure, met with little favor or following in this country. His *Elementa Philosophica,* in which he expounded it, was published by Franklin and used as a text at King's College during the seven years Johnson was at its head, and for a short time thereafter. Otherwise it found little circulation. The Anglican clergy were neither competent nor interested in technical philosophy. The physical scientists, or natural philosophers, like Franklin and Colden, regarded it as merely ingenious and too fantastic. The Puritan theologians whom it might have interested were already provided with the idealism of

Edwards, and besides, they could not tolerate Johnson's Arminian and Anglican propaganda. And as for the schools and academies, they found Paley less original, less provocative, more fashionable, and hence more teachable. Finally Johnson's latter-day enthusiasm for Hutchinsonianism and Hebrew branded him among liberals as a fanatic and served to doom him and his whole philosophy to a venerable oblivion.

One spark, however, caught fire: the reassertion of human agency and freedom. This doctrine became increasingly popular and fed the growing spirit of liberty. Johnson, of course, meant free-will, not free-thought; and moral responsibility, not political liberty; but any idea which defended any freedom was welcomed in those days (as in these) for its liberalism. Above all things Johnson hated liberalism and free-thinking, but he was nevertheless destined to contribute toward it. His advocacy of an American episcopate was regarded in England as a move towards American independence, not towards Anglican loyalty. His attack on the "arbitrary sovereignty" of the Calvinist God, and his defense of God's justice and promises, encouraged the rising tide of sentiment against political forms of arbitrary sovereignty and invincible grace. His opposition to religious strife and enthusiasm helped to create a sober and secular unconcern for religious issues. Above all, his substitution of human happiness for the glory of God as the chief end of man opened the way for the humanitarian revolt against Puritanism.

This most original note in Johnson's *Elementa Phi-*

losophica has received little attention among modern historians, but in his own day, certainly in his own mind, it made a profound impression. His ethics is conceived not in the Puritan terms of the glory of God, but in the rationalistic terms of happiness; and happiness is defined as the complete realization of all the capacities of the soul. There is, first of all, happiness in this life, and then, most important, since the soul is immortal, happiness in the life to come. It never occurred to Samuel Johnson that there was more than a theoretical difference between this heavenly utilitarianism and the traditional conception of man's good consisting in the glory of God. For him, as for the Calvinist, human happiness and the glory of God were identical. Nevertheless the fact that he thought it important to change the terminology has more than a verbal significance. It marks the growing emphasis on humanitarian benevolence, both in human and divine character. The glory of the justice of God, which had impressed Edwards, was repulsive to Johnson, and only because he conceived of God as willing the eternal happiness of all human beings, was he willing to give God the glory. This was the real reason for his dissatisfaction with the philosophy of election and predestination. Johnson's God was a humane God. Therefore no offense to the glory of God is committed when man pursues his happiness even in this world. Man's obligation to seek the salvation of his soul was not for him, as it was for Edwards, the ultimate principle of conduct. This obligation was rather the consequence of man's natural desire for happiness. Johnson, in brief, succeeded in shifting the basis of morals from the sense of sin to the desire for happiness. Though he came to the same practical conclusion as the Calvinist, and though pragmatically the difference seems verbal, it was really fundamental, for the idea of happiness, once admitted, worked like a leaven until, less than a century later, it had overturned the whole system to which Johnson had temporarily reconciled it. Johnson opened the door to human nature, and all that remained to be done was to cancel the eternal part of the soul and eternal happiness, in order to usher in a humanistic, worldly utilitarianism.

At the time when Johnson took this step he was conscious that he was dethroning the sense of sin, but he little dreamed that men would find happiness apart from God. And when he later witnessed the amazing growth of worldliness, of free-thinking, and of preoccupation with the problems of temporal happiness, he began to repent and prayed once more for an awakening of the sense of sin and of the vanity of worldliness. But it was too late, and Johnson himself had contributed largely to the mischief. In a sermon written as early as 1749, almost immediately after his disputes with the Calvinists, we find him emphasizing the "entire dependence of the creature on God" to such an extent that a Calvinist could ask for little more. After proving our utter dependence on the continual operation of God upon our minds for the facts of perception and the truths of reason, he speaks as follows:

"I come now in the last place to consider how in our active powers we depend on God as well as in our powers of perceiving and thinking. And here we must observe that tho' we are intuitively certain from looking into ourselves, that our soul or spirit is indeed a principle of free activity or has a power given it of God of freely exerting and determining itself, yet it depends upon him to assist it in all its exertions, and without his aid its strength is weakness.

"I know it is a notion that very much obtains of late among unthinking or half-thinking people, who know little of themselves and are willing to keep God as much out of sight as they can, to have a strong opinion of their own abilities, and their sufficiency to their own purposes, and consequently in the expressive language of the prophet, to sacrifice to their own net and burn incense to their own dreg. But for my part, the longer I live, the more abasing sense I have of my own weakness and insufficiency to my own happiness, and the more I must account it my greatest glory to depend on God and have recourse to him upon all occasions and in all respects. Nay, I must account it the greatest perfection and happiness of every intelligent creature to depend on a perpetual intercourse with the Deity for all his happiness and all his hopes. I know indeed that I have a self-exerting and self-determining principle, otherwise I could not blame myself if I determine or act amiss. But after all when I find by sad experience how easily we are imposed on and how apt we are to be suddenly surprised and misled, and how weak we are of ourselves to bethink ourselves upon all occasions, to resist the force of appetites or withstand the force of sudden temptation, and how many and frequent the instances are wherein we are surprised into wrong compliances, in a word, when I seriously consider myself as being what I really am, and think of God as being what He really is, I am apt to say with holy Job, nor can I think of a more proper reflection that a creature can make with regard to his almighty creator, in whose hands are his life and breath, and whose are all his ways, Lord, I have heard of Thee, by the hearing of the ear, but now my eye seeth Thee, wherefore I abhor myself and repent in dust and ashes. Nor can I have a greater satisfaction within myself under a sense of my own weakness and impotence than that my soul can make her boast in the Lord, and rejoice to find that all her springs are in Him.

"I know it is a fashionable sort of philosophy (a science falsely so-called) to conceit that God governs the world only by a general providence according to certain fixed laws of nature which he hath established without ever interposing himself with regard to particular cases and persons. Doubtless it is right to be so persuaded of such a general providence, and consequently wrong to be always looking out for particular remarkable interpositions upon every emergency. Notwithstanding which I must believe there is a particular providence that watches over us in all our ways, and that without any sensible varying from the general method of his proceeding in the government of the world, he may and does very often secretly and insensibly influence the minds of men, and lead them to such a determination of their thoughts and resolutions as they would not otherwise have gone into without his influence, and that it is very fit it should be so, as it is of the nature of a creature to be a depending being." [22]

Here he saves enough of the *theory* of human freedom to allow for human responsibility, but to all intents and purposes he admits the dominant power and even the special providence of God, not only in controlling the outward circumstances of man, but even in protecting him from his own passions. He was forced into this attitude not merely by the growth of infidelity in "an apostatising age," but by his personal fortunes as well. In view of his persecution by the Puritans at home and the half-hearted support from the Society in England, which feared that his chief aim, the establishment of an American episcopate, would merely dissolve the last bond between the colonies and the mother-country; in view of the growth of "independent whiggism" in politics and philosophy; and in view of the military successes of the French against the colonies, the poor old Tory had good reason to fear that, unless God definitely intervened, not only his own cause would perish, but England and the colonies would fly to arms and the "House of Bourbon would pick up the remains." In vain he pleaded that

[22] Vol. III, pp. 243-5. *A Sermon on the Entire Dependence of the Creature Upon God* (1749).

the Church could not prosper nor the colonies be saved so long as the candidates for Orders were compelled to undertake the expensive and hazardous journey to London, on which one out of every five perished. When finally his own son, William, on whom he depended to continue his work (his elder son having turned to law), died of the smallpox in London after taking Orders; and when two years later his wife died; and then his son-in-law, who was also one of the mainstays and trustees of the struggling college in New York; and when his second wife died of the smallpox, and he himself was forced to flee into seclusion because of the epidemic, and lived under a continued terror of the disease; when, under these circumstances, he was compelled to abandon his work at the college, with little to show for his labors; and when finally his son, William Samuel, with whom he then made his home at Stratford, was sent to England and kept there for five years as agent for the colony, until the old Doctor began to fear the worst for him too, he was indeed entitled to feel entirely dependent on God, and to be intensely conscious of man's helplessness. His chief comfort now, besides his general trust in a benevolent God, was the idea that these were all signs of the approaching end of the world, and that it was his duty to reawaken a careless and apostatising age to a sense of its sins, before God passed that cruel, irrevocable judgment upon it which it so justly deserved. Had he not been enabled thus to fall back on a sense of sin, it is difficult to see how he could have avoided despair.

Finally, in his anxiety, he broke out into a *Rhapsody,* in which he allows Raphael, the guardian angel or "genius of the English America" to speak words of advice and warning. "[Let] everyone endeavor to possess himself of an habit of the love of human nature, of Christianity, of his country, in general as such as being what are common to all parties, for by this means he would love everyone not as being of this or that or the other party, opinion, or denomination, but as being a man, a Christian, or at least an Englishman."

"Let everyone be upon his guard against high soaring and conceited speculations in matters of religion and using or being imposed upon by words without any meaning, against spiritual pride and conceitedness and affectation of singularity or novelty, and against hard censorious judging one another on account of matters of speculation and private opinion or differences of sentiment or expression in the explication of what all are alike obliged to believe and do. And let Christianity be received as being what it really is, *viz.,* not a system of speculations or fine precise philosophical notions given to gratify the curiosity of inquisitive men, but as a plain practical system designed alike for the whole of the human race and therefore expressed in the language accommodated to the capacities and apprehensions and fitted to the necessities and purposes of the general rate and bulk of mankind; being intended to make them not curious and disputatious but sincerely religious and virtuous and practically wise and good; not to fill their heads with airy notions, but their hearts with holy and heavenly affections and their lives with sober, pure, humble, devout, pious, righteous, faithful, benevolent, and charitable behavior and actions, that they might by this means be qualified for his favor and be as happy as their natures are capable of both here and forever." [23]

The advice of the guardian angel was unheeded. The sense of sin was gone. Americans continued to behave neither like Christians nor Englishmen. Free-thinkers, liberals, Whigs, "new lights" and "independent reflectors" flourished more and more. The Puritan world was crumbling. Johnson attempted to escape from its ruins and sought refuge in the urbane culture, orderly government and worldly wisdom of the Anglican Church and the British nation. But this escape proved impossible in New England. The new forces which were impinging upon American society and thought he failed completely to understand. He did not know that liberty was creating a new religion.

[23] Vol. II, pp. 528, 590. *Raphael, or The Genius of the English America: A Rhapsody.*

CHAPTER VI

THE DECLARATION OF INDEPENDENCE

The growing spirit of self-reliance which gradually undermined Calvinistic piety found its most forceful expression in Jonathan Mayhew. In his student days he had been impressed by the sobriety and tolerance of his father, Experience Mayhew, and of his teacher, the Reverend Ebenezer Gay, of Hingham. Both of them had attempted to remove from Calvinism those elements "which made it difficult of acceptance" and both disliked sectarian bitterness and enthusiasm.

Dr. Gay was an exceptionally scholarly preacher, who introduced his students to the principles of liberal religion, and warned them against substituting their own "sense of Scripture for Scripture itself."[1] In his own preaching he refused to engage in any of the current theological polemics. He even went so far as to say, with the Deists, that "no pretense of revelation can be sufficient for the admission of absurdities and contradictions. The manifest absurdity of any doctrine is a stronger argument that it is not of God than any other evidence can be that it is."[2] And in general he

[1] Ebenezer Gay: *The True Spirit of a Gospel Minister* (Boston, 1746), p. 19.
[2] His Dudleian Lecture at Harvard for 1759, entitled *Natural Reason as Distinguished from Revealed*, p. 22.

argued that "to run down natural religion . . . derogates from the credit of revealed." [3] Following these principles, he sought to break down the sharp antithesis between human freedom and divine grace, between natural goodness and regeneration, between "persevering in the way of duty" and "working out one's salvation." He suggested that the natural conscience of man, whereby God annexes a secret joy to virtuous action, and pain to wrong, acts as a principle of spiritual gravitation. In the moral world man naturally gravitates toward God and finds happiness only in him. Therefore religious faith can rest on the rational foundations of natural morality. In this way Dr. Gay tried to "adjust the devotions of God's people to the dispensations of His Providence." [4]

These ideas testify to the fact that Dr. Gay was studying contemporary English writers. He was, in fact, one of the few of the older clergy who made extensive use of the new shipments of books to the library of Harvard. These shipments began in 1719, when Thomas Hollis, a liberal Baptist in England, donated a large collection of recent authors. Hollis called Mayhew's particular attention to the political philosophies of Locke, Milton, Sidney and Harrington, and to the Deistic theologies of Cudworth, Hutcheson and Clarke. These books worked no less a revolution in the minds of young Bostonians than the Dummer Library at Yale

[3] *Ibid.*, p. 23.
[4] Sermon entitled *The Devotions of God's People Adjusted to the Dispensations of His Providence*, Boston, 1771.

had worked in the minds of Samuel Johnson and his colleagues. Dr. Gay, to be sure, read them with moderation and reserve, for his theological rationalism was tempered by his political Toryism; but young Mayhew and his friends soon became ardent Whigs and enthusiastic liberals both in politics and in religion.

Jonathan Mayhew took his degree from Harvard in 1744, and while the enthusiasm of the Great Awakening was surging about him, he was busy reading Locke and Clarke. Once, while a student, he went to hear Whitefield preach, and wrote about it to his father as follows: "Many persons attended him, but chiefly of the more illiterate sort, except some who went out of curiosity. I heard him once, and it was as low, confused, puerile, conceited, ill-natured, enthusiastic performance as I ever heard." [5] Evidently he felt vastly superior to the "illiterate" enthusiasm of the New Light preachers. He was living in a new intellectual atmosphere to which the old Puritan disputes were largely irrelevant.

It was therefore with reason that both the Old Lights and the New Lights stood aloof when Jonathan Mayhew became minister of West Church, Boston, in 1747. This young man refused to join the Boston Association of Ministers; he established his own series of weekly lectures; he came out frankly as an Arminian, rejected the doctrine of irresistible grace, defended natural religion as a support for revelation, and even laid himself

[5] Letter written in 1749. In Alden Bradford: *Memoir of the Life and Writings of Rev. Jonathan Mayhew* (Boston, 1838), p. 102.

open to the charge of being an Arian or Unitarian.[6] Most shocking of all was his repudiation of doctrinal controversy in favor of discussion of political and moral issues. The Puritan idea of the glory of God was transformed into a moral and social concept. He conceived God as essentially a benevolent ruler, who "governs his great family, his universal Kingdom, according to those general rules and maxims which are in themselves most wise and good, such as the wisest and best kings govern by," and whose "unsearchable wisdom and infinite power, if one may say so, are but the ministers of his infinite goodness, being wholly employed and accomplished in his good and gracious purposes respecting his creatures"; therefore, "perfect goodness, love itself, is his very essence, in a peculiar sense; immeasurable, immutable, universal and everlasting love. And nothing that is in any manner or degree inconsistent with such love has any place in God."[7] It is quite clear that what was "inconsistent with such love" in Mayhew's mind was the doctrine of God's sovereignty and arbitrary grace. Not wishing to become involved in purely theological polemics more than was necessary, he compromised, maintaining that God makes promises to sinners by his own free grace, not because he is bound by justice. But having made promises, God intends to keep them. Therefore there

[6] There is no sufficient evidence that Mayhew openly maintained the Unitarian doctrine, except in the sense that he read much of the current Arian writings in England. He was most influenced by Clarke and the milder Deists.

[7] *Two Sermons on the Nature, Extent and Perfection of the Divine Goodness* (1763), pp. 23-4, 44.

exists a "necessary connection" between man's "striving to enter in at the strait gate" and God's saving grace. Furthermore, Mayhew described such striving, not in terms of enthusiastic seeking, nor in terms of theological strife, but in terms of practical effort, of "wrestling, running and fighting, which express efforts of strength and activity joined with wariness and circumspection." [8] Thus he explains striving to mean moral striving against evil, or actively engaging in the pursuit of good in the face of obstacles. He transformed the idea of salvation into the idea of moral struggle and he reduced the divine glory to divine goodness. [9] He even attempted to prove that God's benevolence is exercised toward each creature severally, that he punishes only "for the common good of the Kingdom," [10] and that "the ultimate design of all the divine commandments is to bring us to a suitable temper and behavior toward each other in order to our mutual happiness." [11]

Not content with dragging his liberal politics into his theology, he dragged particular political issues into the pulpit, such as the question of bishops, the taking of Quebec, the Stamp Act, and *Unlimited Submission and Non-Resistance to the Higher Powers*. The more acute these issues became, the more he insisted on them, until in 1763 he said that true religion comprised the

[8] *Two Sermons on Striving to Enter in at the Strait Gate* (Boston, 1761), pp. 43-4.
[9] See *Two Sermons on the Nature, Extent and Perfection of the Divine Goodness*, pp. 63 ff.
[10] *Ibid.*, p. 67.
[11] *Seven Sermons* (Boston, 1749), p. 141.

love of liberty and country and the hatred of all tyranny and oppression.[12]

Such vigorous propaganda for civil and ecclesiastical liberty well expressed the changing intellectual atmosphere of New England. The people, at least the prosperous traders and lawyers, were no longer conscious of their depravity nor concerned with the economy of redemption; they were asserting natural rights and fighting for worldly interests. And the philosophy which rationalized this tendency came not from Puritanism, but from contemporary English liberalism and Deism. It was a new religion and a new enthusiasm. Many Puritans might have agreed with Samuel Johnson when he referred to "such loose thinkers as Mayhew, who can scarcely be accounted better Christians than the Turks."[13] Whether or not they were Christians, certainly they were not Puritans. They were educated Englishmen fighting for their rights. Through them the prosperous, confident, commercial Yankees discarded the Puritan pretense of their entire dependence on God and transformed their theology into a declaration of independence.

The success of the American Revolution acted as a seal of divine approval on this liberal theology. During the war the clergy were active in patriotic rhetoric and patriotic service. After the war it was impossible for them to revert to their old themes. The spirit of

[12] *Sermons to Young Men* (printed in London, 1767), p. ix.
[13] *Samuel Johnson, President of King's College, His Career and Writings* (New York, 1929), Vol. I, p. 346.

independence, having won its political success, went on to complete its theological conquest.

Jonathan Mayhew died in 1766, at the age of forty-six, but the cause was carried on after the war by his colleague, Charles Chauncy, who was not only a politician active in the cause of the Revolution, but was more of a philosopher than Mayhew. He, too, was well-read in the Deistic theology of the day and was especially influenced by Clarke and Hutcheson, whose conception of God as universal benevolence impressed itself on his mind. A really good God, one who could appeal to sinners, must be infinitely benevolent. "Holiness and purity are inexpressibly beautiful and amiable perfections, but of too bright a glory for sinners to contemplate with delight." [14] Therefore, to make God really delightful and lovable, Chauncy proved him to be "the best as well as the greatest Being in the Universe," [15] the benevolent governor of the cosmic system, whose aim is the greatest good of the system as a whole. In this argument he was careful to point out that God does not aim at the happiness of individuals separately, but at the happiness of the system of which they are parts; and that, since this earth is merely a part of God's good universe, we must not judge God by what he does to this earth or to mankind. Nevertheless, there is sufficient evidence to prove that the particular natural and moral world to which mankind belongs is

[14] Quoted by Chauncy from Clarke's *Sermons,* in the Introduction to his *The Benevolence of the Deity* (Boston, 1784), p. iv.
[15] *Ibid.,* p. iv.

a "good particular whole" [16] and therefore God manifestly aims at the greatest happiness of mankind as a whole. Thus God manifests his glory by being benevolent. "Every creature we cast our eyes upon, discovering pleasure in its existence, from the good it is made capable of enjoying and actually does enjoy is at once an instance and proof of the Divine benevolence." [17]

Chauncy was well aware that such an optimistic, utilitarian deity would seem more plausible to his own Boston congregation, who were actually enjoying the divine benevolence, than to less fortunate sinners, and he explains that some "are dissatisfied with their situation in the world, and quite out of humour, because they don't partake so liberally of the good things of providence, as they imagine they might do. And their discontent is still heightened if they meet with disappointments, and are reduced to suffering circumstances, though by their own folly. And being out of frame, uneasy and restless in their spirits, they find fault with their Maker, and vent themselves in reflections on his goodness; as though it were greatly defective: Otherwise, as they imagine, a more advantageous condition in life might have been allotted to them; and would have been, if the Deity had been as good as they can suppose him to be. These are the complaints, by which the infinitely benevolent Creator, and Governor, of all things, is abused by the less knowing and inquisitive, who are the most numerous: But, as their complaints don't so much originate in judgment, as a

[16] *Ibid.*, p. 58.   [17] *Ibid.*, p. 53.

199

bad temper of mind, this chiefly needs to be rectified, and then their complaints will cease of course." [18] Consequently those who are not aware of the infinite benevolence of God have only their own folly and bad temper to blame. In this way Chauncy accounted for the existence of evil. Originally and naturally the world was created for the happiness of man, but of his own will man corrupted this divine state of nature and brought upon himself the evils of sin and damnation, which were, therefore, not parts of the divine plan but merely human products.

The implications of this theology were revolutionary. The inference, which Chauncy was quick to draw, that the eternal damnation of sinners was inconsistent with God's original plan, had a strange sound in a Puritan pulpit. Chauncy himself hesitated to commit himself to this doctrine. For years he worked secretly on his manuscript, *The Salvation of All Men,* revising it, subjecting it to both philosophical and scriptural authority, and making sure of his ground. In 1782, he published anonymously a pamphlet of extracts from noted writers, entitled *The Salvation of All Men.* It created a sensation immediately; several Calvinists rose to attack it and the "First Presbytery of the Eastward" in session at Windham, Connecticut, published a volume against "Origenism, or the doctrine of universal salvation, as lying nearest the root of all the impiety and wickedness now leading the fashion in

[18] Chauncy: *The Benevolence of the Deity* (Boston, 1784), p. v.

places of public resort." [19] On the other hand the doctrine was so evidently fashionable among the liberals, and had been for years quietly harbored by so many Congregationalists, that Chauncy took courage and published, in 1784, his *Salvation of All Men, the Grand Thing Aimed at in the Scheme of God,* by "One who wishes well to the whole Human Race." The book opens with the sentence: "The whole human race are considered in the following work as made for happiness."

These words clearly express the spirit of the Revolutionary generation in America. The pursuit of happiness and the exercise of benevolence were henceforth not merely the secular aims of a new nation, they were embedded in the "Scheme of God," the essential attributes of Deity. The moral revolution in New England from Puritanism to Americanism transformed God from the Perfect Being of Edwards into the Universal Benevolence of Chauncy. One is reminded of the dramatic shift in Plato's *Symposium* when Socrates announces that love is not a god but a search for pure beauty. The reverse shift took place in the mind and society of New England: Puritan benevolence or love had found its object in the excellence and glory of God; now benevolence itself was deified. This profound change in theology was a frank, though tardy, recognition of the change in morals. Or, to use the words of Dr. Gay, "the dispensations of God's provi-

[19] Joseph Henry Allen and Richard Eddy: *A History of the Unitarians and the Universalists in the United States,* Vol. X in the American Church History Series (New York, 1894), p. 386.

dence" were at last "adjusted to the devotions of his people." Like his people, God had become devoted to human happiness and to that kindly benevolence which "constitutes us worthy objects of eachother's love, and lays the foundation for that mutual trust between man and man, without which there could be no such thing as public happiness." [20] God himself had become republican.

The cradle of this theological liberty was the Harvard Library, and its champions came almost exclusively from "the favored sons of this Seminary." [21] The rank and file of the Congregational and Presbyterian clergy throughout New England, and even more throughout New York and New Jersey, feared what they called the latitudinarian tendencies of Harvard.[22] But since Boston was the headquarters of political liberty, and since political liberty was preached throughout the land, the liberals of Boston and vicinity were able to preach their humanistic and deistic doctrines without fear of serious opposition. And thus it happened that the historic homes of Puritanism became the hotbeds of revolt, and the very pulpits which once defended the sovereignty of God now rang with the praises of reason, rights and freedom. The heat of the Revolution naturally encouraged excesses of pulpit

[20] Chauncy: *The Benevolence of the Deity* (Boston, 1784), p. iii.
[21] *Cf.* Alden Bradford: *Memoir of the Life and Writings of Rev. Jonathan Mayhew* (Boston, 1838), p. 185.
[22] Of course, free-thinking among the laity was prevalent throughout the colonies, especially in Philadelphia and the South, but there was little liberalism among the clergy elsewhere until the days of Priestley.

oratory, and these habits, formed during the war, maintained themselves for a generation; so that long after the rest of the clergy had settled back into comfortable habits of thought, the Boston group were still on the rampage. We read, as late as 1809, that "the clergy of Boston are little better than Deists. . . . Those very men who in New York and Philadelphia would probably be infidels because they could not be Calvinists, are among us in Boston, rational Christians; the most constant supporters of public worship, the most intimate friends of the clergy, and not a few professors of Christianity." [23]

The best illustration of this extreme tendency is the Rev. William Bentley of Salem.[24] The old town which had been the storm center of Puritanism became after the Revolution a peaceful and prosperous community of merchants. Many of them travelled into the Far East and brought back their tales of oriental life and thought. Quite a few were Freemasons, whose membership in this international fraternal body served to protect them from the pirates. Their contacts with the French and other Europeans during the Revolution had also made them hospitable to radical ideas. One of them, for example, Timothy Pickering, began to doubt his Puritan theology when he heard General von Steuben say that he would sooner believe in an

[23] Letter of Joseph Buckminster to Thomas Belsham. See John Williams: *Memoirs of the Late Rev. Thomas Belsham* (London, 1833), pp. 593-4.

[24] See unpublished manuscript in the Columbia University Library by Melba P. Wilson: *Pre-Revolutionary Liberalism and Post-Revolutionary Unitarianism in America* (1930).

absurdity than in the Trinity.[25]   To these worldly-wise
merchants Dr. Bentley preached a radically republican
gospel.   He was himself unusually learned, even for a
Harvard graduate, and his learning embraced not only
theology but secular literatures in many languages,
questions of politics and political economy.   He was a
Freemason, a unitarian and universalist, a distinguished
journalist and an ardent admirer of Jefferson and his
republican philosophy.

The gospel which he preached at Salem may be sum-
marized as follows: "For what good ends Christians
have shaken the foundations of their own religion by
depreciating natural religion may not be easy to determine. . . . Natural religion is still the most excellent religion." [26]   "How much more pure the charity
of a savage than the pulpit-anathemas of a priest against
churches which differ from his own." [27]   God be-
friended Israel that he might use them to promote
universal religion, and although Mohammedans and
Jews may err in detail, their devotion, zeal and obedience are certainly acceptable to the Universal Father
of all.   Religion leads us to consider ourselves "not of
small societies only . . . but as belonging to the house-
hold of the faithful who dwell in every nation and in
every clime with one God and Father who hateth
nothing that he has made, but loveth and cherisheth

[25] See Bernard Fay: *The Revolutionary Spirit in France and America:
a Study of the Moral and Intellectual Relations between France and the
United States at the End of the Eighteenth Century* (New York, 1927),
p. 470.
[26] *Sermon Preached at Stone Chapel* (Boston, 1790), p. 17.
[27] *Ibid.*, p. 15.

it." [28]   By natural religion the will of God is made known to us and Christianity only assists us in the further knowledge and practice of it. Revelation acts merely in an auxiliary capacity until "a variety of causes, wisely fitted to act, may render this assistance unnecessary. . . . The Son himself shall then be put under, and God by perfecting human nature, be all in all." [29] "Heaven and happiness were not designed by God as the exclusive rights of learned priests or ingenious doctors; they are the end which God had proposed for all mankind, and are therefore by the same means, attainable by all men." [30] Happiness is not only the reward of virtue, but it is the end for which we have been created. Often earthly circumstances seem not to correspond to a design of immediate good, but through knowledge, the evil consequences of the decrees of Heaven which can not be changed, can at least be avoided. It is therefore education that promotes the greatest usefulness and happiness. Through the development of the social principle in him, man will discover other means of overcoming evil, even the evils of society, itself. For he will discover that in his social loyalty lies his own security and well-being. [31] Through an awakened social consciousness, men will develop their imaginations to see remoter needs; and through the established laws and institutions of society,

[28] *Ibid.*, pp. 22-3.
[29] *Ibid.*, p. 18.
[30] *Ibid.*, pp. 8-9.
[31] See William Bentley: *Sermon occasioned by the Death of Jonathon Gardner, Esq.* (Salem, 1791), p. 19.

through education, through inquiry into specific abilities, and through mutual aid, they will realize a more permanent good than the sporadic efforts of disunited individuals could ever attain.

No faith could be further removed from Puritanism than this whole-hearted humanitarian and social gospel. Further south and coming from a layman, this doctrine might have caused little alarm; but coming from the minister of Salem, it was an eloquent tribute to the growth of what the Puritans called infidelity. To be sure, Dr. Bentley was the exception and not the rule; he was a Jeffersonian Democrat in a land of Federalists, but he indicated the popular drift. In his diary we have a graphic account of what was taking place in Boston as well as in Salem. He wrote in 1795: "The congregation belonging to the New North Church was much changed since my attendance in it in youth. The galleries were less crowded and partly removed. The assembly was chiefly on the floor, which is large. There are not more houses on the north end of Boston than fifty years ago, but they are differently filled. The two Anabaptist societies and the Universalists have thronged galleries, and the lowest class of people neglect public worship." [32] In 1802 he made similar observations: "The members of the present New Brick Assembly complain of the small number [of attendants]. The galleries are entirely forsaken, which have not for forty years been full. . . . In this part of

[32] *The Diary of William Bentley, D.D., Pastor of the East Church, Salem, Massachusetts, 1784-1810.* 3 vols. (Salem, 1905-1911), Vol. II, p. 127.

the town the largest house and assembly is in the New North, which has much less number in the gallery than formerly, tho' full upon the pews below." [33] He continued to say that the Bennett Street Meeting House was crowded with Universalists, and that the First and Second Baptist Churches were filled. "The Baptists by attaching themselves to the present administration, have gained great success in the United States, and greater in New England than any sect since the settlement, even beyond comparison. This seems to be a warning to the churches of the older denominations. . . . The Congregationalists begin to be alarmed at the great progress of the Anabaptists, but the progress is not from their opinions, but from their political situation to oppose the busy clergymen who are tools of the anti-Jefferson party. The controversial books will be little read, unless to make bigots on one side, and to strengthen opposition; and oppression will make more friends for the Anabaptists among those who despise their opinions and their sect." [34]

In short, while the elect were gathered in their handsome pews, listening to the Puritan gospel, the people of the galleries were deserting the faith of their fathers and crowding to hear the more hopeful message of universalists and republicans. Puritanism had become perfectly genteel.

[33] *Ibid.*, Vol. II, p. 425.
[34] *Ibid.*, Vol. II, p. 418. *Cf.* also Vol. III, p. 82, or the same opinion expressed in 1804.

CHAPTER VII

THE DECLINE AND FALL

The story of how these ideas gradually undermined the Puritan philosophy, and how the followers of Jonathan Edwards defended their ground inch by inch against increasing odds, takes us into one of the most intricate and pathetic exhibitions of theological reasoning which the history of Western thought affords. The dialectic involved is so replete with apparently meaningless technical distinctions, and the literature of the movement is so controversial in spirit, that the few theologians who have taken the pains to pick their way through this desert have merely succeeded in convincing others that there are no signs of life in it. And modern Protestants are so thankful to be rid of the Puritan incubus that they point to these post-Edwardeans as the death agony of a monstrous theology which should never have been born. But though the theological terms of the debate are hopelessly antiquated, and though the cause of Puritanism is certainly dead, the issues and motives which dominated the struggle are still alive. Other men are fighting with other weapons for the same ends; it may be possible for a kindly, clinical observer to see in this story, as in a mirror, the perennial interplay between moral ideals and dialectical justification, between faith and reason. And if he looks closely he will see how reason, once it has lost its foundation in faith, makes desperate resistance, but must eventually surrender to those physical forces which govern all forms of life and death.

Not long after the Great Awakening, the Reverend Joseph Bellamy, of Bethlem, Connecticut, who had studied with Edwards at Northampton and had engaged in itinerant evangelical preaching, took an aggressive stand by publishing his *True Religion Delineated or Experimental Religion Distinguished from Formality on the One Hand and Enthusiasm on the Other, Set in a Scriptural and Rational Light in two discourses, in which some of the principal errors both of the Arminians and Antinomians are confuted, the foundation and superstructure of their different schemes demolished and the Truth as it is in Jesus explained and proved. The whole adapted to the weakest capacities and designed for the establishment, comfort and quickening of the people of God in these evil times.*[1] This was the beginning of a serious effort on the part of Edwards' disciples to defend the faith against increasingly "evil times." Jonathan Edwards, Jr., continued at Princeton, later at Union. The other leaders of this group came from Yale: Joseph Bellamy, Samuel Hopkins, Nathanael Emmons, and Timothy Dwight. President Ezra Stiles was himself a very influential figure, though he was less of a theologian. The move-

---

[1] Boston, 1750. In *The Works of Joseph Bellamy, D.D. . . . with a Memoir of his life and character* [by Tryon Edwards] (Boston, 1850). Subsequent references to the *Works* are to this edition.

ment was, in short, an attempt by Yale men to stem the tide of "latitudinarian tendencies" emanating from Harvard.

In 1750, Bellamy followed Jonathan Edwards' example and repudiated the Half-Way Covenant both in theory and practice. In a series of dialogues published in 1768 between a minister and a parishioner he justified his stand. The parishioner is a typical church member of the time—sincere, conscientious, but withal unregenerate. In fact, he has no conception of what the Covenant of Grace implies. He wants to know what he must do to have his child baptised, and he receives the simple answer that he must "give himself to the Lord." Somewhat abashed, the parishioner then argues that he never intended to be a member in full communion, and admits: "I merely meant to 'own' the Covenant, as the phrase is, and have my child baptized, but I had no design to profess godliness or to pretend to a real compliance with the Covenant of Grace. This godly people may do; but it had been great hypocrisy in me to do it." [2] "Accordingly I never met with the church when they had church meetings upon church business. . . . I never voted when the church were called to give their vote in any matter whatsoever. Nor had I any right to go to the Lord's table." [3] "But I can at least with moral sincerity promise to walk in his ways . . . and I am persuaded that God has made

[2] *The Half-Way Covenant* (New Haven, 1769), p. 9. *Works,* Vol. II, p. 672.
[3] *The Sacramental Controversy Brought to a Point. The Fourth Dialogue,* etc. (New Haven, no date), pp. 16-17. *Works,* Vol. II, p. 705.

the Lord's Supper a converting ordinance . . . and
when men of sense and conscience find themselves
denied the enjoyment of ordinances for themselves and
children in our churches they will turn to the Church
of England."⁴ To all these considerations, which sum-
marize the current arguments against strict Puritanism,
the Minister has ready answers in terms of the Covenant of Grace. It is not enough to profess "moral
sincerity" or an "endeavor" to obey or a "desire" to give
oneself to God. The Covenant demands "holy obedience" proceeding from the love of God and "avouching
the Lord Jehovah to be your sovereign Lord." Since
God requires only this declaration of love and devotion,
since it is merely a matter of "the heart," there is no
excuse for doubting or hesitating: "Come for all things
are now ready." He who hesitates to make this choice
thereby reveals his lack of grace and all his talk about
moral striving is evidence that he has no spontaneous
love of God. Bellamy elsewhere clinches his argument
with an analogy:

"Thus it is also when persons enter into the marriage
covenant: they see their way clear to act, by looking,
each one, into his own heart, and finding such affections in themselves, as are answerable to the external
transaction before them. . . . Should a few women
object against this covenant, and publicly propose an
alteration, saying, 'we pray, that the words, *loving,
faithful and obedient* may be left out, for the sake of
some young *women of tender consciences,* who cannot

⁴ *The Half-Way Covenant,* pp. 6-7. *Works,* Vol. II, pp. 687-90.

see their way clear to use them.' The only question would be this, 'Ought alteration to be made in the marriage covenant, or in the young women?' Or in other words, 'which is wrong, the woman's heart, or the covenant?' A question, which may easily be decided, if we appeal to reason or to scripture: but if we appeal to corruption, the more we wrangle, the more we may. Some might say, 'if the covenant is not altered, no woman can be married without full assurance. For it is not lawful to enter into this covenant in doubt. For *he that doubteth is damned*. An infallible assurance therefore is necessary. But who has this? Or what woman on this plan, can be married with a good conscience? And, besides, what priest can be able to judge, whether any are fit to be married? By what rule shall it be certainly known, when a woman is really disposed to be a loving, faithful and obedient wife, and when she is not? Moreover, it will only tempt bad women to make a lying profession, while women of tender consciences will be kept back; and those who are married will grow proud because they are judged to be qualified. Meanwhile, the failings of married women will be more taken notice of, to their dishonor, for using this covenant. Upon the whole, it is a very bad plan, and a thing of a very dangerous tendency; therefore, we propose, that in all future times, these words, *loving, faithful, obedient,* be left out of the marriage covenant.'—How ridiculous would any woman make herself, that should advance such stuff! But if this class of women were the majority, they might make a shocking noise, but there would be no more sense in it, than if but one single woman was in the scheme." [5]

The issue was simple in Bellamy's mind because it was only a question of holy love. One either loves or not—there is no room for either effort or doubt; it concerns only "the heart," and the heart reacts immediately. Love is spontaneous, whole-hearted and uncalculating; otherwise it is not genuine. "The more unable to love God we are, the more are we to blame." [6] But love has always been more complicated in practice than in theory, and Bellamy was compelled to witness the prevalent reluctance to love God, though he could not understand it. His preaching, in fact, consisted of painting the glory of God to sinners, in the hope that they could not resist Him; and thus he hoped to win the unregenerate. He relied much on his evangelistic preaching, not because it was theoretically a means of grace, but because it enabled sinners to see God. For all practical purposes, therefore, the "unregenerate doings" carried on by Bellamy, though they were not to be regarded as means of grace, were identical with the "strivings" preached by Mayhew and other liberals as necessarily leading to entrance into the strait gate. There was a real danger that God's freedom and sovereignty would be compromised by human doings, and

---

[5] *That there is but One Covenant . . . namely, The Covenant of Grace, proved from the Word of God; And the doctrine of an Extreme Graceless Covenant . . . shown to be an unscriptural doctrine* (New Haven, 1769). *Works*, Vol. II, pp. 502-3.

[6] *True Religion Delineated*, Discourse I, Sec. III. *Works*, Vol. I, p. 100.

that the divine privileges of the churches would be opened to "awakened and enlightened sinners" instead of being retained for God's elect in the Covenant of Grace.

Samuel Hopkins came to the rescue with a distinction. He proved that it was morally impossible for a sinner to desire to enter the strait gate and that therefore all strivings and doings of the unregenerate merely dragged them deeper into the pit of self-reliance and self-salvation. The most hardened sinner is he who imagines that he can oblige God to save him on account of his natural virtue. God will not be obliged! Man must surrender unconditionally; and no man is further from surrender than he who is still confident of the value of his own strivings. "The plain reason for this is, his sin and guilt are infinite and his virtue finite. Therefore the latter . . . is of not more avail . . . than nothing at all." [7] It follows that "the secure, unawakened sinner does not sin so directly and immediately against God as the awakened, convinced sinner." [8] Such an extreme statement of the Puritan doctrine of sin and grace was repulsive even to those who wanted to be good Calvinists, though it was the inevitable implication of their logic. And the reason Hopkins was ready to insist on it was that he introduced a distinction

[7] Samuel Hopkins: *The Knowledge of God's Law Necessary in Order to the Knowledge of Sin* (Boston, 1768). In *The Works of Samuel Hopkins, D.D. . . . with a Memoir of his Life and Character* by Edwards S. Park (Boston, 1854), Vol. III, p. 534, note. Subsequent references to the *Works* are to this edition.

[8] *The True State and Character of the Unregenerate, etc. . . . being a reply to Mr. Mills's "Inquiry . . ."* (1769). *Works*, Vol. III, p. 309.

which put the whole question in a new light. Since an infinite sinner is wholly at enmity with God, a person who is actually striving for salvation must have experienced an act of divine grace antecedently, which made it possible for him to strive. Therefore those who strive have reason to believe that they are no longer technically unregenerate and that the Holy Spirit has already performed an immediate, instantaneous and imperceptible work of regeneration on their hearts. Their striving is not a means *to* grace, but an evidence *of* grace, and the goal of striving is not regeneration (which is antecedent and immediate), but sanctification and justification which are the eventual fruits of "holy exercises" and virtuous living. The practical value of this distinction is obvious: unassured or merely striving persons could claim to be regenerate without being conscious of any work of grace on their souls; they could rely on circumstantial evidence of what is in itself imperceptible. Awakened sinners were thus practically equivalent to striving saints. They could be accepted as church members and members of the Covenant of Grace, but they could nevertheless be encouraged to moral effort as a means to justification. God's freedom in dispensing grace was reconciled with man's use of means; both means and end were maintained without being necessarily related to each other.

By thus distinguishing between regeneration and justification, Hopkins was able to maintain Bellamy's emphasis on change of heart, but the "new heart" became a mere phrase since the change was imperceptible. He was careful to explain that any change in a man's mind was subsequent to this regeneration of heart: hence no sinner could rely on "speculative knowledge" of God to save him. The new heart is a means to new light, not *vice versa*. The value of mental enlightenment, and of the so-called means of grace, is in the exercise of Christian holiness *within* the Covenant, and since the object of regeneration is holiness, God as a matter of fact does not waste his grace on the benighted who would not know how to use it profitably. But this is merely a matter of policy on God's part, not a matter of promises to enlightened sinners. "God can, doubtless, as easily change the heart of the most ignorant, deluded Mahometan, or heathen, yea, the most blind, stupid Hottentot in the world, as that of the most awakened, enlightened sinner under the gospel. But if he should do so by the regenerating influences of his Spirit, there could be no right and proper exercises of Christian virtue and holiness; because such a one is without any right speculative knowledge of those truths, in the view of which alone Christian holiness is exercised. And giving a new heart, or a right taste and temper of mind, would not remove this darkness. . . . Therefore, we have no reason to think God ever does so." [9]

Such clever dialectics saved the day for the churches: the strict Covenant of Grace was maintained, but en-

[9] *An Inquiry Concerning the Promises of the Gospel*, Sec. X, "Of the Ends and Design of Means" (1765). *Works*, Vol. III, p. 266.

trance into the Covenant was made a purely formal and technical act; divine election was as essential as ever, but it carried with it no claim to moral superiority or holiness; and the means of grace could be restricted to the elect. The infinite depravity of the unregenerate was compatible with their moral enlightenment; and the change from sinner to saint was made immediate and imperceptible, for the benefit of those persons of tender consciences who did not wish to appear godly hypocrites. Hopkins had personal evidence that he had solved the problem for the Puritan churches. His relentless Calvinism had led in 1769 to his dismissal as minister to the poor people at Great Barrington;[10] the following year he was invited to the fashionable church of Newport, Rhode Island, where he lived happily to a good old age, free from the annoyances of unregenerate doings, for there he could rely on a congregation of the elect. But he threw consternation into the camp of the theologians. Both liberals and Calvinists feared "the new theology": it was too difficult, too fine-spun, and no one was sure where it would lead. It stimulated endless controversy in theology, but meanwhile it had prolonged the life of the Covenant.

Unfortunately others soon succeeded in making the problem of church membership as complicated as Hopkins had made theology. In 1767 the Reverend Moses

[10] His theology was only one of a number of factors which caused his dismissal. Ironically, he was a Whig in politics and was opposed by many wealthy Tories in Great Barrington, so that his poor friends were no longer able to support him.

Hemmenway, of Wells, Massachusetts, had preached *Seven Sermons on the Obligation and Encouragement of the Unregenerate to Labour for the Meat which endureth to Everlasting Life,* in which he defended "unregenerate doings" against the Hopkinsonians, and inclined somewhat toward the position of Mayhew. Twenty-five years later, in 1792, he published a treatise which offered a practical reconciliation by making a whole series of technical distinctions. It was entitled, *A Discourse concerning the Church; In Which the Several acceptations of the Word are explained and Distinguished; the Gospel Covenant delineated; A Right of Admission and Access to Special Ordinances, in their outward administration and inward efficacy, Stated and Discussed. Designed to Remove the Scruples and reconcile the Differences of Christians.* Hemmenway revived the distinction between visible and invisible saints, and between the external, or Church Covenant, and the internal, or Covenant of Grace, and he asserted the principle that the church, even in the matter of access to communion, is concerned not with the *reality* of grace, but with the *evidence* of grace. This doctrine led him to distinguish between "relative," "federal" or "covenant" holiness on the one hand, and inherent holiness on the other. The former is not merely the external appearance of the latter, but is a distinct kind of holiness which characterizes visible saints. Both visible and invisible saints have a right to full communion, but the invisible must, in addition, give external evidence of inherent holiness. Therefore there are two kinds of visible saints, those possessed of external evidence of inherent holiness and those possessed of external federal holiness, and both kinds are entitled to the privileges of full communion.

Nathanael Emmons then replied in behalf of the strict Calvinists.[11] He admitted that external evidence was sufficient to entitle a person to membership in the church, but that access to the communion was a matter of conscience and concerned not the external evidence but the internal reality of grace. This interpretation threw the whole problem into the air again. Emmons apparently intended it to relieve ministers from the responsibility of deciding who was entitled to communion, but it revived all the old issues in a new form: Is membership merely external? Is real grace merely internal? Is the sacrament a seal of the Covenant of Grace, or an external means of grace? How can members know that they are real saints? And what is the relation between appearance and reality in general?

For Emmons the evidence of real grace was external, since the internal reality was, according to him, a matter for God, not the churches, to judge. Therefore he emphasized the moral consequences of regeneration and tried to counteract the imperceptible and "mechanical" regeneration preached by Hopkins. This moralistic emphasis on Emmons' part had been carried still further by the Reverend William Hart, of Saybrook. He regarded regeneration as a gradual process, not a

[11] *A Dissertation on the Scriptural Qualifications for Admission and Access to the Christian Sacraments: comprising some strictures on Dr. Hemmenway's Discourse concerning the Church* (Worcester, Mass., 1793).

sudden endowment, and he even went so far as to argue that men were transformed *through* the power of the gospel; in other words, that the means of grace were in themselves efficacious. Above all, he resented the harsh attitude taken by the Hopkinsonians towards unregenerates. "It is greatly to be wished," he wrote, "that all who have the office of teachers of religion to others would learn of Jesus Christ to give an honoring representation of his Father's more than paternal kindness and love towards man and breathe Jesus' compassionate tenderness towards poor perishing sinners in their doctrine." [12]

To this Nathanael Whitaker, the champion of spiritual regeneration, replied: "Such a way of flattering sinners may engage their affections to their minister, but does not lead them to a sense of their entire wretchedness without Jesus Christ." [13] Here the practical issue clearly came to a head: shall the ministers preach the popular gospel and thus "engage the affections" of their congregations, or shall they revive the strict theory of the Covenant and the sense of sin and thus make the great majority "wretched without Christ." The argument became increasingly *ad hominem* as the theology became hopelessly artificial. Each attempted refinement in the doctrine of the Covenant made the whole philosophy of redemption more tech-

---

[12] William Hart: *Brief Remarks on a Number of False Propositions and Dangerous Errors, which are spreading in the country; . . . written by way of Dialogue* (New London, 1769), pp. 49-50.
[13] Nathanael Whitaker: *Two Sermons: On the Doctrine of Reconciliation* (Salem, 1770), p. 117.

nical. Emmons thought he was introducing clarity and precision when he defined visible saints as "those who appear to profess real holiness." [14] But how about those who profess apparent holiness, or those who are apparently but not professedly really holy, or those who really appear merely to profess holiness, or those who neither appear nor profess to be holy but really are? Emmons thought that so long as members *appeared* to be *really* holy, the church had no right to inquire further into their souls. But does *real* holiness ever *appear*? The good Doctor tried to help the Puritans out of a practical difficulty; he succeeded in launching American epistemology. Timothy Dwight, then President of Yale, foresaw this danger and tried to retreat. He repudiated the refinements of Emmons, returned to the comparatively harmless immediate, instantaneous and imperceptible operation of grace as expounded by Hopkins, as well as to Bellamy's evangelical concern for unregenerates and their doings. But the damage was done and the Puritan theologians had become so involved in the intricacies of their systems that they carried on an endless controversy about appearance and reality, while the churches were forced to turn to more practical business and to more humane preachers—a division of labor between philosophy and religion which is still prevalent.

It is clear that what chiefly undermined the idea of regeneration was the unwillingness of church members

---

[14] *A Dissertation on the Scriptural Qualifications for Admission and Access to the Christian Sacraments,* p. 51.

to profess godliness, and what made them unwilling to do so was the fact that godliness was coming to mean less an act of election in the divine mind determining the cosmic status of a soul, and more a quality of conduct in human affairs. When the declaration of grace ceased to signify a sort of divine initiation ceremony and became a profession of moral integrity, it became stultifying. The unregenerate, being sinners, naturally did not possess the good grace to interpret such professions charitably; they looked upon professed saints as holier-than-thou persons, and hence as hypocrites. The social odium thus attached to self-confessed regeneration was sufficient to destroy it. The growing force of secular morality, or, as it was then called, of natural religion, induced a failure of nerve in the whole Calvinistic theology. It became increasingly necessary to defend dialectically doctrines which were actually losing credibility.

The consequent degradation of Puritan theology from an expression of faith into a system of apologetics is more readily sensed than proved, for though the impending doom is evident on every page, the exact points of yielding are difficult to detect. Retreats are notoriously reported as strategic consolidations, and lost causes always perish victorious. No Calvinist was ever more confident of his position than Samuel Hopkins, yet his very assurance betrayed at bottom the hysteria of despair; his proof was so perfect that, when it failed, all was lost. As long as Jonathan Edwards was alive, his various vindications of Calvinism were enlivened by the fact that his theology was the formulation of a genuine *credo,* the fruit of a profound experience. After him its successive defenses became increasingly apologetic, for they upheld a formal *creed,* the plausibility of which had to be preached. Edwards believed what he said; Hopkins said what he thought ought to be believed.

In 1757, Jonathan Edwards wrote his remarkable treatise, *The Great Christian Doctrine of Original Sin Defended.* His argument was based on commonplace facts which the liberals freely ignored. He pointed out that our various acts, whether of virtue or of sin, are not isolated events but expressions of an underlying character. Habitual benevolence or depravity, as the case may be, is the determining factor in human conduct and the successive choices or acts are not absolute in themselves, but evidences of the character or constitution from which they proceed. If this is true in individual conduct, it is also true of human nature in general. We are not independent wills, but children of Adam, sharing a common constitution with our fellow human beings. We are sinners by origin; not because Adam's sin is imputed to us, but because Adam's fall was typical or representative of human nature in general. This natural unity of man was called by Edwards God's moral constitution. In Adam, our federal head or representative, all men sin: God does not blame us for Adam's act of sin, he damns us for being, like

Adam, subject by nature to sin. Here Edwards is at his best and his Calvinism is impregnable.

But trouble began in that same year, 1757, when an anonymous pamphlet appeared under the innocent title, *A Winter Evening's Conversation upon the Doctrine of Original Sin*.[15] The author paid slight attention to the usual theological arguments, but proceeded to bewail the fate of damned infants: "How can you reconcile it to the goodness, holiness or justice of God to make infants heirs of hell and send them into the world only to breathe and die and then take them away, or even send them to hell from their mother's womb before they have seen the light of life? What! make them first to open their eyes in torments; and all this for a sin which certainly they had no hand in.
. . . And all this from the holiest, justest and kindest being in heaven and earth! Mayn't we venture to say it is impossible!"[16] "O good father of heaven and earth, what doleful apprehensions must they have of this thine excellency and glory, who can suppose that thou shoulds't pronounce a sentence by which myriads of infants, as blameless as helpless, were consigned to the blackness of darkness to be tormented with fire and brimstone for ever . . . taking up the innocent helpless millions and shaking them awhile over that habitation of devils, just ready to cast them into it,

[15] Written by Samuel Webster of Salisbury, Mass. The full title is: *A Winter Evening's Conversation upon the Doctrine of Original Sin . . . wherein the notion of our having sinned in Adam and being on that account* ONLY *liable to eternal damnation is proved to be unscriptural, irrational, and of dangerous tendency* (New Haven, 1757).
[16] *Ibid.*, pp. 5-6.

while they know not their right hand from their left!"[17] The very rhetoric which Edwards had on occasion used to convert the unregenerate is here turned effectively against him. All his arguments were useless in the face of this pathetic plea, and everyone felt instinctively: Infant damnation? Impossible!

Peter Clark, A.M., minister at Danvers, replied with *A Summer-Morning's Conversation*,[18] in which he admitted that "the great Christian doctrine of original sin" is indeed "most disagreeable to the proud heart of man"; but he ventured to hope that God has found some humane way of dealing with damned infants and he asserted that "few or none maintain" that infants must suffer the torments of hell-fire. He then attempted to justify his belief that God deals differently with infants and with mature sinners, though He "has not thought fit so far therein to gratify our curiosity as to acquaint us with the method of his dealing with infants." He distinguished between conscious depravity and the mere principle of sinfulness. The former is positive depravity and merits the torments of hell; the latter is merely the imputed corruption of Adam and merits eternal death.

Such intellectual timidity toward the onslaughts of sentimentality was, of course, quickly seized upon by

[17] *Ibid.*, p. 24.
[18] *The Scripture Doctrine of Original Sin, Stated and Defended. In A Summer-Morning's Conversation between a Minister and a Neighbour. Containing Remarks on a late anonymous pamphlit, intitled, "A Winter-Evening's Conversation . . ."* (Boston, 1758).

the liberals. Chauncy pointed out [19] that Clark was giving the case away for Calvinism, and that not only the punishment of infants but the whole notion of eternal punishment in general was inconsistent with the divine goodness. This forced the Edwardeans in justifying their theory of punishment to justify a world in which infinite punishment was necessary. Accordingly, in 1759, Samuel Hopkins wrote his bold tract, *Sin through Divine Interposition an Advantage to the Universe,* and the following year, Bellamy published *The Wisdom of God in the Permission of Sin.*

Bellamy's argument opened in a grand manner, submitting a formal proof that the sinful world is the best of all possible worlds: "In the days of eternity, long before the foundation of the world, this system, now in existence, and all other possible systems, . . . all equally lay open to the divine view, and one as easy to Almightiness as another. He had his choice. He had none to please but himself; beside him there was no being. He had a perfectly good taste, and nothing to bias his judgment, and was infinite in wisdom: this he chose; and this, of all possible systems, therefore was the best, infinite wisdom and perfect rectitude being judges. If, therefore, the whole were as absolutely incomprehensible by us as it is by children of four

---

[19] *The Opinion of one who has perused the Summer Morning's Conversation, concerning Original Sin, wrote by the Rev. Mr. Clark . . . in a letter to a friend* (Boston, 1758). See the title page and pages 13-6, *passim.*

years old, yet we ought firmly to believe the whole to be perfect in wisdom, glory, and beauty." [20]

Such formal optimism was as harmless as it was unconvincing, but when Bellamy began to elaborate the structure of this system, his optimism was soon taken to be ironical. He explained that "herein consists the wisdom of God in the affair, not in bringing good out of good, but in bringing infinite good out of infinite evil"; [21] and the infinite good turned out to be the infinite punishment of infinite evil. Bellamy did not mince words: "To view the vindictive Justice of the Divine Nature, as a Beauty in the Divine Character, is to see that all heaven ought forever to love and adore the infinitely glorious Majesty, for punishing Sin according to its desert. And unless it appears to us a beauty in the divine conduct thus to punish sin, we shall be at enmity against his whole plan of government." [22] By this argument Bellamy took the offensive against those liberals who professed to be defending the justice of God. He frankly adopted the theory which Grotius had developed and which had become one of the strongholds of Deism, namely, that God is not an arbitrary sovereign but a moral governor of the universe, and that God's chief end is to exhibit the perfection of the moral law. In this way Bellamy tried

[20] Joseph Bellamy: *The Wisdom of God in the Permission of Sin* (Boston, 1760), Sermon II, p. 7. *Works,* Vol. II, p. 28.

[21] *The Wisdom of God in the Permission of Sin Vindicated* (Boston, 1760). *Works,* Vol. II, p. 119.

[22] *An Essay on the Nature and Glory of the Gospel of Jesus Christ: as also on the Nature and Consequences of Spiritual Blindness and the nature and effects of Divine Illumination* (Boston, 1762), p. 235. *Works,* Vol. II, p. 439.

to transform the medieval idea of ransom, redemption and pardon into the moralistic categories of eighteenth-century rationalism: justice, constitutional government, and moral law.

According to this theory Christ's atonement consists in his revelation of obedience to the law, his willingness to undergo the wrath and punishment of God; and his mission was not so much that of redeeming man from sin as of demonstrating the infinite evil of sin. Christ's death is therefore to be regarded as a proof primarily of God's justice and only secondarily of his love. "If vindictive justice is a glorious and amiable perfection, then it was a glorious and amiable Thing in God to bruise Him and put His soul to grief, who had espoused our Cause, and appeared as our Representative, although he were his own Son. And it was a glorious Thing in the Son of God incarnate to say Thy Will be done. But if vindictive Justice is not glorious, there is no glory in the Cross of Christ. And where no Glory is, no Glory can be seen. If vindictive Justice is an amiable, glorious Perfection, then the Grace of God in the Gift of his Son was free Grace indeed. . . . Therefore those who are wholly blind to the beauty of Vindictive Justice are wholly blind to the Nature and Glory of the Grace of the Gospel. And therefore, that Idea of free Grace, which ravishes an Antinomian Heart is a mere imagination, formed of his own Fancy, and not the true Grace of the Gospel."[23] Here the traditional story of redeeming love

[23] *An Essay on the Nature and Glory of the Gospel of Jesus Christ*, etc., p. 103. *Works*, Vol. II, p. 348.

is translated into a praise of strict justice. Christ is glorified because he upheld the moral law, and he becomes, like Adam, our federal representative before God.

Thus to exalt vindictive justice, at a time when the liberals were preaching a benevolent God, was, of course, exceedingly unpopular doctrine. It is not enough that a man love God's benevolence; he must admire the beauty of God's infinite hatred of sin. The moral law of God is as excellent as his grace. The fact that men find it difficult to believe this is sufficient evidence of their depravity. "The more unable to love God we are, the more we are to blame."

Samuel Hopkins took a slightly different direction in his treatise, but succeeded in making the doctrine even more unpalatable. He compromised the sovereignty of God by the "moral government" theory to the extent of being "willing to leave the word, decree, out of the question . . . as it is a word that is become hateful and frightful to many." [24] But he insisted that God's sovereignty is no whit impaired by the fact that his will is not arbitrarily decreed, and sin is merely "permitted."

"God acts in the highest sense and degree as a sovereign; he being, not only under no obligation to grant such a favour to anyone, when he does it; but there is in the sinner, something infinitely contrary to this, even infinite unworthiness of the favour granted, and

[24] Hopkins: *Sin Through Divine Interposition an Advantage to the Universe* (1759, printed Boston, 1773). *Works,* Vol. III, p. 530.

desert of infinite evil. Therefore, whenever God changes and regenerates the heart of a sinner, he does what he was under no sort of obligation to the sinner to do; but might justly leave him to the hardness of his own heart, to perish in his sins for ever. So that God in determining to whom he will grant this infinite favour, and in giving it to some, and withholding it from others; 'has mercy on whom he will have mercy; and whom he will he hardeneth.' What the sinner does before he is regenerated, does not lay God under any degree of obligation to him, by promise, or any other way. For he complies with none of God's commands or offers, in the least degree. He is not so much as willing to accept of offered mercy; but opposes God and his grace with all his heart, however anxious he may be about his eternal interest, and how much soever he prays and cries for mercy: and continues a perfect enemy to the just God and the Saviour, until his heart is renewed, and the enmity slain by the regenerating influence of God's Spirit." [25] Hopkins even went so far as to attribute a "disinterested malice toward God" to every "natural" man. He was forced into this unreal psychology by his attempt to reject the motive of self-love absolutely. Seeing that the liberals, and even some of the most orthodox, were smuggling into theology the popular conceptions of self-love, of regard for one's own eternal happiness, and in general of devotion to the public good as a means of

---

[25] *The Cause, Nature, and Means of Regeneration* (Boston, 1768). *Works,* Vol. III, p. 566.

promoting private good, Hopkins determined to preach the *disinterested* love of God's glory with a vengeance. And *per contra* he insisted that the opposite of loving God is not self-love, but *disinterested* malice toward God.[26]

The more such doctrines were insisted on the more incredible they became, for the moral and political ideas on which the theology was modelled were rapidly becoming antiquated. After the American Revolution, and certainly after the French Revolution, it was idle to build a theology in terms of sovereignty, vindictive justice, and free grace. These concepts had become socially obsolete and therefore Calvinism had no moral basis to which it could appeal. Hopkins naturally made some attempt at adaptation, and he tried, as Bellamy did, to justify God's permission of sin. Though he did not admit that perfect benevolence demanded God's concern for the ultimate happiness of all human beings, he believed that God aimed at the "greatest general good of the universe," and he attempted an elaborate proof that the consequences of sin contribute to the general "advantage." To introduce utilitarian considerations into the argument, and to show in detail how God brings good out of evil and how infinite good brought out of infinite evil demonstrates a higher · perfection in God than an eternally and automatically happy world, was, of course, a considerable concession to liberal ways of thinking. Charles Chauncy was quick to detect this fact and took the opportunity to

[26] See *An Inquiry into the Nature of True Holiness* (Newport, 1773).

suggest that on the basis of "advantage to the universe" it is difficult to justify eternal punishment. God must have some end in punishing sinners, but endless punishment must be aimless.

Such universalistic exploitation of his doctrine forced Hopkins to retreat in the direction of Edwards. He pointed out that punishment is not utilitarian in the pedagogical sense, and that God does not punish sinners in order to reform them. Hell is chastisement, not chastening. Punishment is useful only in the sense that it exhibits the heinous nature of sin, and hell must be infinite because sin is infinite by nature. The punishment must fit the crime.[27] God's moral honor compels him to insist on infinite punishment for infinite evil. By this argument Hopkins was able to defend Calvinism against the humanitarian sentiments of Chauncy, but in so doing, he had robbed God of most of his glory. There was a certain majesty in Edwards' and Bellamy's conception of the divine being who hates evil and "curses" sin. For them hell represented the holy wrath and curse of God. For Hopkins, God's majesty had dwindled into a moralistic and legalistic defense of his "honor" and preoccupation with punishment for its own sake. The righteous indignation of God had degenerated into a vindictive delight in punishing helpless sinners eternally. From this absurdly cruel conception, Calvinism never recovered. Jonathan Edwards, Jr., tried to improve on it by suggesting that

[27] Hopkins: *An Inquiry Concerning the Future State of Those Who Die in Their Sins; or, endless punishment consistent with divine justice, wisdom, and goodness* (Newport, 1783).

such punishment really "promoted the public good of God's constitution," [28] but this sop to current republicanism merely aggravated the incredibility of the doctrine. Timothy Dwight finally succeeded in making a burlesque of it by his theory that sinners continue to sin endlessly in hell and hence their punishment must go on forever.[29] Such arguments transformed the doctrines of God's glory and man's depravity from profound philosophical ideas into petty theological quibbles and centered attention on the literal details of the torments of damned infants and on the boundless cruelty of endless punishment. When the defense of the moral order became so inhuman, no amount of logic could save it. The more the doctrine was proved, the less it was believed.

As a result, the humanitarians did not need to use logic; they could count on public sentiment. A few sentences from William Ellery Channing are sufficient to prove the intense reaction against Puritanism which buried not only the post-Edwardean theologians but Edwards himself beneath a wave of "respect for the human soul." "From the direction which theology has taken, it has been thought that to ascribe any thing to man was to detract so much from God. The disposition has been, to establish striking contrasts between man and God, and not to see and rejoice in the

[28] Edwards: *The Salvation of All Men Strictly Examined* (New Haven, 1789).
[29] Timothy Dwight: *Duration of Future Punishment* (New York, no date).

likeness between them. It has been thought that to darken the creation was the way to bring out more clearly the splendor of the Creator. . . .

"God, we are told, must not be limited; nor are his rights to be restrained by any rights in his creatures. These are made to minister to their Maker's glory, not to glorify themselves. They wholly depend on him, and have no power which they can call their own. His sovereignty, awful and omnipotent, is not to be kept in check, or turned from its purposes, by any claims of his subjects. Man's place is the dust. The entire prostration of his faculties is the true homage he is to offer God. He is not to exalt his reason or his sense of right against the decrees of the Almighty. He has but one lesson to learn, that he is nothing, that God is All in All. . . .

"If Edwards's work on the Will could really answer its end; if it could thoroughly persuade men that they were bound by an irresistible necessity, that their actions were fixed links in the chain of destiny, that there was but one agent, God, in the universe; it would be one of the most pernicious books ever issued from our press. Happily it is a demonstration which no man believes, which the whole consciousness contradicts. . . .

"Let it not be imagined from these remarks, that I would turn the mind from God's Infinity. This is the grand truth; but it must not stand alone in the mind. The finite is something real as well as the infinite. We must reconcile the two in our theology. It is as dangerous to exclude the former as the latter. God surpasses all human thought; yet human thought, mysterious, unbounded, 'wandering through eternity,' is not to be contemned. God's sovereignty is limitless; still man has rights. God's power is irresistible; still man is free. On God we entirely depend; yet we can and do act from ourselves, and determine our own characters. These antagonistic ideas, if so they may be called, are equally true, and neither can be spared. It will not do for an impassioned or an abject piety to wink one class of them out of sight. In a healthy mind they live together." [30]

With Channing, the religion of self-reliance is upon us. Contradictions lived side by side in his admittedly healthy mind and failed to trouble him. The Puritan doctrines were not repudiated, they were merely subordinated; they were admitted but not really believed. They had become harmless halos appropriated by a new faith for the sake of keeping up appearances. For these self-confident Unitarians were not required to build their own churches, they inherited the meeting houses of the Puritans, together with their social traditions and intellectual habits. They became in turn the elect and they wore their Puritan halos with the customary New England pride and dignity.

Even the latter-day Calvinists themselves were content to make this compromise. Timothy Dwight became an ardent patriot and nationalist, preaching the

[30] William E. Channing: *The Works of William E. Channing, D.D.* (Boston, 1898), pp. 2-4, "Introductory Remarks."

new gospel of social solidarity and progress. He carried the principles of "natural religion" as far as he could, but he always kept the Calvinistic framework in his system, so that he could fall back on what he called "the mediatorial system" when the faith was in danger. After Dwight, Nathaniel W. Taylor softened Calvinism still more, until by the middle of the nineteenth century Puritan theology had wholly lost its sting and its power.

CHAPTER VIII

UNGODLY PURITANS

Not long after the appearance of Cotton Mather's *Essays to Do Good,* the readers of the *New England Courant* were startled by the satirical articles of one Mrs. Silence Dogood. She agreed with the Reverend Mr. Mather that doing good was the most important business of life; but she made it her business to expose evil in high places. She began by attacking college life among the "scollars" at Harvard; then she reprimanded their parents for sending them merely to display their own wealth; then she made fun of the theological debates and pretensions of the professors. The fashionable clergy came in for their share of moral treatment by Mrs. Dogood, and even the magistrates and members of the council were not spared. Such essays to do good were not exactly to the Mathers' taste and, when James Franklin, the editor of the *Courant,* and Silence Dogood, whose real name was Benjamin Franklin, continued in their efforts despite warnings, fines and imprisonment, their journal was finally suppressed.

Removed to Philadelphia, Benjamin continued to "do good." When he organized his Junto Club there, he inserted among the rules of procedure the following paraphrases of Cotton Mather's proposals: "Have you lately observed any encroachment on the just liberties of the people? What new story have you lately heard agreeable for telling in conversation? Have you lately heard of any citizen thriving well, and by what means? Do you think of anything at present, in which the Junto may be serviceable to mankind, to their country, or to themselves?" Between these queries there was a pause "while one might fill and drink a glass of wine," in place of Cotton Mather's pause "that any member may offer what he pleases upon it."

In all this there was evidently an element of sheer wit and playfulness. Franklin had caught the spirit of Addison and Steele's *Spectator,* of Defoe's *Essays,* and in general of the free-thinking, satirical literature of his day. In company with his young deistic friends, first in Boston, then in Philadelphia, and later in London, he enjoyed the free play of radical ideas. During his first sojourn in London he published a tract *On Vice and Virtue,* which proved that on the premises of God's attributes of wisdom, goodness, and power, one is forced to conclude that "vice and virtue are empty distinctions." A few years later he used the same sort of reasoning on prayer and predestination. Franklin's own summary of it appeared in a letter to Vaughan in 1779. "Almost all men, in all ages and countries, have at times made use of prayer. Thence I reasoned, that, if all things were ordained, prayer must among the rest be ordained. But, as prayer can procure no change in things ordained, praying must be useless, and an absurdity. God would therefore, not ordain praying, if everything else was ordained. But praying exists, therefore all things are not ordained, &c." [1]

At first, in his eagerness to be counted one of the clever deistic intellectuals, he concluded from such considerations that morality did not exist. In care-free fashion he exploited the arguments of both Calvinists and Deists. He wrote a *Dissertation on Liberty,* one on *First Principles,* and some *Dialogues Concerning Virtue and Pleasure.* These pieces all reveal a fondness for pushing an argument to its limits; they are not moralistic but sheer free-thinking. Soon, however, Franklin abandoned this speculative and playful tone and emphasized the more serious implications of the business of doing good. He discovered that the arguments in which he and his comrades indulged were merely continuing the bad intellectual habits of the theologians. Here is his own confession and condemnation of his early disputatious habits: "We sometimes disputed, and very fond we were of argument, and were desirous of confuting one another—which disputatious turn is apt to become a very bad habit, making people often disagreeable in company, by the contradiction that is necessary to bring it into practice; and thence, besides souring and spoiling the conversation, it is productive of disgusts, and perhaps enmities, with those who may have occasion for friendship. I had caught this by reading my father's books of dispute on reli-

[1] See I. W. Riley: *American Philosophy. The Early Schools* (New York, 1907).

gion. Persons of good sense, I have since observed, seldom fall into it, except lawyers, university men, and generally men of all sorts, who have been bred at Edinburgh." [2]

From this it appears that one reason why Franklin abandoned dialectical and theological disputes was his desire to be well-mannered. He noticed that "positiveness" and "direct contradiction" were not in good taste in polite conversation. Accordingly he disciplined himself and imposed fines on members of the Junto who committed these violations of good manners.

There is a more serious reason, however, for Franklin's so-called conversion from Deism. His own hard experiences and his whole New England training convinced him that vice and virtue were "no empty distinctions" and that the theologies and metaphysics which made them appear such were therefore futile. This discovery he mentions in the *Autobiography* with his characteristic simplicity. "I grew convinced that truth, sincerity, and integrity, in dealings between man and man, were of the utmost importance to the felicity of life." [3] He realized that the liberal theologians and the city churches were relaxing from the gospel of work and discipline which the Puritans had preached during the generations of strenuous building, and were becoming acclimated to the habits of luxury and leisure. The spirit of work was giving way to the theology

[2] *Autobiography.* In *The Complete Works of Benjamin Franklin,* compiled and edited by John Bigelow (New York, 1887-8). Subsequent references to the *Works* are to this edition unless otherwise noted.

[3] *Autobiography. Works,* Vol. I, p. 139.

of having arrived, and the clergy were degenerating
into a disputatious crowd of theocrats. Meanwhile
more secular workers were exemplifying the strenuous
virtues of the early Puritans. In this situation, Benjamin Franklin made the attempt to maintain the
Puritan virtues in all their rigor, but to abandon entirely their theological sanctions. He placed the frontier morality on a utilitarian footing, and gave it empirical foundations. The whole issue he put in a few
words: "Revelation had indeed no weight with me,
as such; but I entertained an opinion, that, though
certain actions might not be bad, *because* they were
forbidden by it, or good, *because* it commanded them;
yet probably these actions might be forbidden *because*
they were bad for us, or commanded *because* they were
beneficial to us, in their own natures, all the circumstances of things considered." [4] What Franklin said
was simply: If you want to achieve anything, these
old-fashioned Puritan virtues are the necessary means:
temperance, silence, order, resolution, frugality, industry, sincerity, justice, etc. And if you ask for proof,
Franklin could point to his own experience and to the
colonies themselves as evidence.

What is designated as the Benjamin Franklin morality is probably too familiar to require detailed description. A few of Franklin's own words give its chief
outlines. As a young printer in Philadelphia, he wrote
the following: "Those who write of the art of poetry

---

[4] *Autobiography. Works,* Vol. I, p. 139. This was, of course, not an
original discovery with Franklin. Samuel Clarke and other Deists had
emphasized it.

teach us that, if we would write what may be worth reading, we ought always, before we begin, to form a regular plan and design of our piece; otherwise we shall be in danger of incongruity. I am apt to think it is the same as to life. I have never fixed a regular design in life, by which means it has been a confused variety of different scenes; I am now entering upon a new one; let me, therefore, make some resolutions, and form some scheme of action, that henceforth I may live in all respects like a rational creature.

"1. It is necessary for me to be extremely frugal for some time, till I have paid what I owe.

"2. To endeavor to speak truth in every instance, to give nobody expectations that are not likely to be answered, but aim at sincerity in every word and action; the most amiable excellence in a rational being.

"3. To apply myself industriously to whatever business I take in hand, and not divert my mind from my business by any foolish project of growing suddenly rich; for industry and patience are the surest means of plenty.

"4. I resolve to speak ill of no man whatever, not even in a matter of truth; but rather by some means excuse the faults I hear charged upon others, and, upon proper occasions, speak all the good I know of everybody." [5]

From his famous chapter on "The Art of Virtue" in the *Autobiography,* I quote the following: "In the

[5] *Autobiography,* footnote in the chapter on "The Art of Virtue," in *The Works of Benjamin Franklin,* edited by Jared Sparks (Boston, 1840), Vol. I, p. 105.

various enumerations of the moral virtues I had met with in my reading, I found the catalogue more or less numerous, as different writers included more or less under the same name. Temperance, for example, was by some confined to eating and drinking; while by others it was extended to mean the moderating every other pleasure, appetite, inclination, or passion, bodily or mental, even to avarice and ambition. I proposed to myself, for the sake of clearness, to use rather more names, with fewer ideas attached to each, than a few names with more ideas and I included under thirteen names of virtues, all that at that time occurred to me as necessary or desirable; and annexed to each a short precept, which fully expressed the extent I gave to its meaning.

"These names of virtues, with their precepts, were:

"1. Temperance—Eat not to dulness; drink not to elevation.

"2. Silence—Speak not but what may benefit others or yourself; avoid trifling conversation.

"3. Order—Let all your things have their places; let each part of your business have its time.

"4. Resolution—Resolve to perform what you ought; perform without fail what you resolve.

"5. Frugality—Make no expense but to do good to others or yourself; that is, waste nothing.

"6. Industry—Lose no time; be always employed in something useful; cut off all unnecessary actions.

"7. Sincerity—Use no hurtful deceit; think innocently and justly; and, if you speak, speak accordingly.

"8. Justice—Wrong none by doing injuries, or omitting the benefits that are your duty.

"9. Moderation—Avoid extremes; forbear resenting injuries so much as you think they deserve.

"10. Cleanliness—Tolerate no uncleanliness in body, clothes or habitation.

"11. Tranquility—Be not disturbed at trifles, or at accidents common or unavoidable.

"12. Chastity—Rarely use venery but for health and offspring, never to dulness, weakness, or the injury of your own or another's peace or reputation.

"13. Humility—Imitate Jesus and Socrates.

"My intention being to acquire the habitude of all these virtues, I judged it would be well not to distract my attention by attempting the whole at once, but to fix it on one of them at a time; and when I should be master of that, then to proceed to another; and so on, till I have gone through the thirteen. And, as the previous acquisition of some might facilitate the acquisition of certain others, I arranged them with that view, as they stand above.

"It may be well posterity should be informed, that to this little artifice, with the blessing of God, their ancestor owed the constant felicity of his life. . . . To Temperance he ascribes his long-continued health, and what is still left to him of a good constitution; to Industry and Frugality, the early easiness of his circumstances and acquisition of his fortune, with all the knowledge that enabled him to be a useful citizen, and obtained for him some degree of reputation among the learned; to Sincerity and Justice, the confidence of his country, and the honorable employs it conferred upon him; and to the joint influence of the whole mass of the virtues, even in the imperfect state he was able to acquire them, all that evenness of temper, and that cheerfulness in conversation, which makes his company still sought for, and agreeable even to his young acquaintance." [6]

In *The Way to Wealth,* which is a compilation of the best of his sayings as "Poor Richard," [7] Franklin's moral doctrine takes this more popular form: "It would be thought a hard government that should tax its people one tenth part of their time, to be employed in its service: but idleness taxes many of us much more; sloth, by bringing on diseases, absolutely shortens life. 'Sloth, like rust, consumes faster than labour wears, while the used key is always bright,' as poor Richard says. 'But dost thou love life, then do not squander time, for that is the stuff life is made of,' as poor Richard says. How much more than is necessary do we spend in sleep! forgetting that 'the sleeping fox catches no poultry, and that there will be sleeping enough in the grave,' as poor Richard says.

"If time be of all things the most precious, wasting

[6] *Works,* Vol. I, pp. 174-7. This prayer is also taken from the *Autobiography:* "O powerful Goodness! bountiful Father! merciful Guide! Increase in me that wisdom which discovers my truest interest. Strengthen my resolution to perform what that wisdom dictates. Accept my kind offices to Thy other children as the only return in my power for Thy continual favors to me." *Works,* Vol. I, p. 181.

[7] The form and substance of his maxims were suggested to him by various authors. See the excellent discussion of this point in Bernard Faÿ: *Franklin, The Apostle of Modern Times* (Boston, 1929), pp. 30 *ff.* and 158 *ff.*

time must be, as poor Richard says, 'the greatest prodigality'; since, as he elsewhere tells us, 'lost time is never found again, and what we call time enough always proves little enough': let us then up and be doing, and doing to the purpose; so by diligence shall we do more with less perplexity. 'Sloth makes all things difficult, but industry all easy; and he that riseth late, must trot all day, and shall scarce overtake his business at night; while laziness travels so slowly that poverty soon overtakes him. Drive thy business; let not that drive thee; and early to bed, and early to rise, makes a man healthy, wealthy, and wise,' as poor Richard says.

"Methinks I hear some of you say, 'must a man afford himself no leisure?' I will tell thee, my friend, what poor Richard says; 'employ thy time well, if thou meanest to gain leisure; and since thou art not sure of a minute, throw not away an hour.' Leisure is time for doing something useful; this leisure the diligent man will obtain, but the lazy man never; for a life of leisure and a life of laziness are two things. Many, without labour, would live by their wits alone, but they break for want of stock; whereas industry gives comfort and respect. 'Fly pleasures, and they will follow you. The diligent spinner has a large shift; and now I have a sheep and a cow, everybody bids me good-morrow.' "

Philosophers are offended by the simplicity, almost simpleness, of this morality. Surely there can be nothing profound in a doctrine which a Pennsylvania farmer could understand. Though more recent instrumentalists have succeeded in putting this doctrine in language which appeals more to "university men, and generally men of all sorts that have been bred at Edinburgh," any analysis of intelligence usually reveals the validity of Franklin's contentions; and though it may be more systematically developed and more elaborately conceived, the implications for conduct will be substantially the same. Certainly no method of presentation of utilitarian ethics could have been more effective than Franklin's, for he is to this day the patron saint of those who are interested in achievement.

Franklin's mind is typical of an easy, spontaneous hospitality to ends or ideals, and of an intellectual preoccupation with their practical challenge. Pennsylvania needed fortification against the French and Indians; Franklin began at once to work on plans for organizing a militia and buying cannon. In view of their common interests against Great Britain, the colonies wanted some sort of union; Franklin immediately proposed a plan. Throughout his life, he was continually proposing plans—a plan for the promotion of abolition of slavery, a plan for bringing the comforts of civilization to the natives of New Zealand. The "art of virtue" was simply one more plan. Any end, suggested to his mind, immediately raised the problem of its accomplishment. He even told the great evangelist, George Whitefield, how he could most easily convert great numbers of people, advising him to convert a few popular leaders, "grandees," first and then the masses would follow. "For," said he, "men fear less the being in hell than out of fashion." [8] In his scientific researches, too, practical problems seemed to stimulate him most. I do not mean practical applications like the lightning-rod, for these were of minor concern to him, but rather problems of designing apparatus, of experimental conditions for testing hypotheses, and of methods for dealing pragmatically with rival hypotheses. His inventions are further evidence of this habit of mind—an improved harmonica of vibrating glasses, bi-focal spectacles, smokeless fireplaces, to say nothing of his electrical devices. It would be difficult to find a mind more given to free play in the objects of its interests, yet more intent on their practical aspects.

In this preoccupation with instrumental values, Franklin is typical of what Europeans call "Americanism," and the objection usually made to Franklin's moral philosophy, and for that matter to any other utilitarian ethics, is that it is merely instrumental. "You tell us," the criticism runs, "the 'way to wealth,' but you fail to tell us whether or not wealth is a good. You tell us how to succeed in business, but you fail to tell us whether or not our business is worth while." The more superficial critics of Franklin (to say nothing of the critics of utilitarianism and pragmatism) immediately infer that "material prosperity" is the admitted end. To them Franklin is merely a typical American business man who, without stopping to evaluate, simply adopts the business principles of thrift for thrift's sake, money for money's sake, the more the

[8] *Works,* Vol. II, p. 151. Letter of July 6, 1749.

better. That this is not true of Franklin's personal life is easily proved. As soon as he became "free and easy" he quit his business and devoted himself to science, literature, public affairs, and conversation with his friends,—pursuits which from boyhood had been his chief delight. As early as 1748 he wrote to Cadwallader Colden: "I am in a fair way of having no other tasks than such as I shall like to give myself, and of enjoying what I look upon as a great happiness, leisure to read, study, make experiments, and converse at large with such ingenious and worthy men as are pleased to honor me with their friendship or acquaintance, on such points as may produce something for the common benefit of mankind, uninterrupted by the little cares and fatigues of business." [9] And a year later he wrote to his mother: "At present I pass my time agreeably enough. I enjoy, through mercy, a tolerable share of health. I read a great deal, ride a little, do a little business for myself, now and then for others, retire when I can, and go into company when I please; so the years roll round, and the last will come, when I would rather have it said, 'He lived usefully,' than 'He died rich.'" [10] A further example of this attitude is found in his speculations on "raising a United Party for Virtue." The successful demonstration of his "art of virtue" on himself suggested to him the possibilities of its social and political application. Members of this United Party, "good and wise men" of all nations, were

[9] *Ibid.*, Vol. II, p. 115. Letter of Sept. 29, 1748.
[10] *Ibid.*, p. 154.

to discipline themselves in accordance with the program Franklin had earlier followed himself. They were to be called "The Society of the Free and Easy. Free, as being, by the general practice and habits of the virtues, free from the dominion of vice; and particularly, by the practice of industry and frugality, free from debt, which exposes a man to constraint, and a species of slavery to his creditors." [11]

Mr. D. H. Lawrence's criticism of Franklin's table of virtues [12] rests entirely on his presupposition that they are final, not instrumental virtues. If they are taken as the ends of life, they are easily satirized. Lawrence himself seems to fall into the trap which he lays for Franklin in that he tries to re-define these purely disciplinary virtues in such a way as to give them ideal content. The result is even more ridiculous than it is intended to be. Justice, for example, he re-defines as follows: "The only justice is to follow the sincere intuition of the soul, angry or gentle. Anger is just, and pity is just, but judgment is never just." [13] This is obviously no definition of justice at all. It may be a definition of freedom. Lawrence was so preoccupied with the praise of freedom, of individuality, of mastery, of imagination, of his gods, in short, of the ideal or final values of life, that it never occurred to him that Franklin could be talking about something quite different. Franklin's table of virtues is not a catalogue of his ideals or objects of worship, and to attempt to read

[11] *Autobiography. Works,* Vol. I, p. 191.
[12] In his *Studies in Classic American Literature* (New York, 1923).
[13] *Ibid.,* p. 26.

ideal content into them is Lawrence's, not Franklin's, mistake. Franklin was just as much interested in being "free and easy" as Lawrence was—more so, in fact, for he was willing to work towards it. No one can blame Lawrence for protesting against the popular confusion of means and ends, and the general tendency to make God an "everlasting Wanamaker," but his reading this into Franklin himself is not excusable. Lawrence seems to have had a fairly keen appreciation of ideals, but none whatsoever of morals; Franklin had some of both. "Early to bed and early to rise, makes a man healthy, wealthy and wise." Health, wealth and wisdom, is not a bad summary of the final goods of human life. But none of them occur in Franklin's table of virtues; it is concerned exclusively with the "early to bed and early to rise" side of life. Lawrence had no room for this instrumental side of life in his philosophy, but one suspects that even he, as a matter of practice, applied considerable "resolution, frugality, industry and sincerity" to the writing of his books, though, as an artist, he had the good taste not to talk about it.

In Franklin's philosophy, as well as in his personal life, therefore, a sense of values is evident, values of which he did not lose sight, and in the service of which his moral philosophy was merely and precisely an instrument. Franklin was not interested in establishing his Puritan discipline as an end in itself. He assumed that people have ends, that they want to be "free and easy," and that they understand wealth as merely the necessary means for enjoying the real ends of leisure society. The reason "wealth" and similar terms figured so largely in Franklin's writings was simply that the people for whom he was writing thought in those terms. Any term which symbolized the ends for which people actually were striving was welcome to Franklin. He made no attempt to prescribe the ends which men should follow.

Franklin's attention was as consistently confined to the concrete analysis of means as the attention of the Greeks to ends. Aristotle made explicit what any Greek would have admitted to be a life well lived. The greatness of his ethics rests on the fact that the Greek virtues,—balance, wisdom, beauty, and the rest, —are commonly admitted ends. Franklin's virtues,— frugality, industry, sincerity, honesty, and the rest,— are not ends. It was the glory of the Greeks that they persisted in painting perfection in the face of practically minded objectors, with their, "But how is this possible in a barbarian world?" It was the greatness of Franklin, on the other hand, that he refused to abandon his Puritan principles because they were disagreeable. The decline of Puritan morals symbolizes less a growing tolerance of natural goods, or a discovery of better methods of attaining them, than an impatience at being obliged to work for them. The freedom, leisure and beauty which we enjoy are obviously the fruit of generations of discipline and even of slavery, and while we do well to point out the slavishness of those Puritans who make discipline an end in itself, we are in danger of the folly of imagining that we can achieve beauty without labor. The Greeks took slavery for granted. We, too, would be nearer the facts of life if we took slavery for granted, than we are when we imagine that Puritan virtues are antiquated. They are as universal in morals as the Greek ideals are in art. Their truth is as old as history and quite proverbial. It was understood long before Franklin, but seldom has it been stated so concretely, so simply, and so empirically. The hypothetic form of these maxims is indicative of their scientific character. They do not dictate, they advise. Franklin does not say, "thou shalt and thou shalt not." He says, *"if* you would be healthy, wealthy and wise, you must go early to bed and be early to rise; *if* you would be free and easy you must cultivate the art of virtue; etc." Judgments in this form are about matters of fact and can be put to empirical tests. Not being bound to a particular set of standards, such an inquiry can discover the physical conditions of any. An ethics of means is, therefore, akin to the sciences, as an ethics of ends is to the arts. Artists are engaged each in his own individual work, but the instruments with which they ply their arts may be common. Or, in Franklin's own terms, the art of virtue may be useful to anyone for whom life is an art.

Franklin's table of virtues, inasmuch as it is not a philosophy of human ideals, is to be regarded neither as a substitute for the Aristotelian ethics, nor as a glorification of bourgeois commercialism in the face of the

chivalry of the feudal aristocracy. If the Franklin
morality substitutes for anything, it is for the traditional
Christian virtues, for they, too, constitute a philosophy
of the discipline of life. The Christian life is traditionally portrayed as one of humility, charity, penitence,
poverty, self-denial, a forgiving spirit. These are obviously instrumental virtues and not ideal perfections,
for they disappear in heaven. This traditional code
of the feudal ages proved ill-adapted to the pioneer life
of New England. Consequently the Puritan virtues, in
spite of the fact that they were sanctioned by a Christian theology, were not traditionally Christian. The
contrast between the Yankee and the saint, as types
of character, is familiar enough. The two philosophies
involved are practical alternatives. Franklin, in the
Autobiography, explicitly retracts humility, the chief
of the Christian virtues, as impractical; he said he found
that when he was humble he was proud of his humility,
and he admitted that he had hastily inserted humility
as the thirteenth virtue in his table on the advice of a
Quaker who told him that he "was generally thought
proud." [14] Franklin's diagnosis of his own case cor-
responds fairly well to the historians' diagnosis of Puritans in general. They pretended to live saintly lives,
but their actual ideals were pagan. They pursued
"health, wealth and wisdom" while they professed election into the Covenant of Grace. Franklin saw clearly
the growing incompatibility between the morals prac-

---

[14] Compare Jonathan Edwards' remark that he was not content to be
merely humble to the dust as other sinners are, but infinitely humble!

ticed and the morals preached, and he changed the preaching.

There was a brief time in Franklin's life when he concerned himself more or less seriously with religious reform. He tried to work out in detail a religious system which would give sincere expression to his moral ideas. He wrote down the rudiments of a theology, composed prayers, and while in England he even undertook, with Lord le Despencer, to revise the English Prayer Book.[15] For various reasons he soon abandoned this project. To a certain extent Freemasonry and his Junto Club were his substitutes for churches. But above all he dropped religious subjects in order not to stimulate one more theological controversy. He made it a policy to disturb no one in his religious practices and beliefs; he supported various religious institutions and he apparently became a good friend of both Whitefield and Samuel Johnson. Thus he made his peace with all religions and devoted himself to none. And while theologians were struggling, as we have seen, to revise Christian ideas to meet changing American morals, Franklin was free to take the other alternative. He reasserted the stern Puritan morality, but divorced it from the theocratic aims which it originally served.

In his austere moralism, Franklin was undoubtedly a Puritan, however much he may have revolted against Calvinism. His "art of virtue" is in significant contrast

[15] On this subject, see Phillips Russell: *Benjamin Franklin, The First Civilized American* (New York, 1926), Chapters X and XXIV, esp. pp. 224-6.

to the liberal temper and popular radicalism of his day and it can not be regarded as the product of his contacts with European civilization, nor of his Freemasonry, nor of his admiration for Sir Roger de Coverley. In other ways Franklin was no doubt a typical eighteenth-century man of the world, but as a moralist he was a child of the New England frontier. Jonathan Edwards and Benjamin Franklin thus represent the two opposite poles of Puritan thought. It was Edwards who attempted to induce New England to lead a godly, not a sober, life; it was Franklin who succeeded in teaching Americans to lead a sober and not a godly life.

Having stepped beyond the literal confines of our subject by introducing Benjamin Franklin as the classic incarnation of Puritan pioneering, we can not close our story without telling of the resurrection of Puritan piety in the mind of Nathaniel Hawthorne. For it would be unjust to Puritan theology to give the impression that it was buried utterly by Edwards' disciples. As Franklin translated into secular terms the moral discipline of New England, so Hawthorne translated into empirical truths the essential doctrines of Calvinism.

Though Hawthorne's life might be used to illustrate Franklin's philosophy—a career of faithful plodding crowned eventually by leisure, success and happiness—his mind was the perfect opposite of Franklin's. Practical problems bored him, physical needs fretted him, and social life disgusted him. Labor he regarded as "the curse of the world." [16] The noisy commercialism of Salem, the cheap politics of the Whigs, and the childish romanticism of the Transcendentalists, were all contemptible to him. He lived out of season. The Hathornes were a proud old sea-faring family of Salem, who insisted on maintaining their Puritan gentility to the bitter end. Nathaniel's mother and sister kept themselves undefiled by the contemporary world. They lived indoors with their ancestors. Nathaniel himself grew up under the habit of regarding himself and his family as far superior to their townspeople. His imagination dwelt in Old Salem, when the gloom of his own home was still the dominant atmosphere of the town, when the elect were still respected and life still had a serious meaning. He professed to hate his Puritan heritage but he never scorned it; his scorn was reserved for his contemporaries. Though he was sociable enough with a few chosen companions, drinking and playing cards with them, he refused to take them seriously or share ideas with them.

Emerson naturally felt Hawthorne's aloofness most keenly, for he could not understand how his neighbor could be so cold toward his ideas, when all the world was paying homage to them. And it is more or less directly to Emerson that we owe the conventional picture of Hawthorne—secluded, solitary, sceptic. To an enthusiastic, self-reliant idealist Hawthorne would, of course, appear thus, but now that others besides

[16] From a letter quoted in Lloyd Morris: *The Rebellious Puritan: Portrait of Mr. Hawthorne* (New York, 1927), p. 135.

Hawthorne have become sceptical of Emerson's philosophy, it is time to lay off the transcendentalist spectacles and look at Hawthorne through uncolored lenses.

On the surface he appears to be holding up Puritanism for ridicule, or at least for hatred. The grim *Twice-told Tales*, the dingy *House of the Seven Gables*, and the tragic *Scarlet Letter*, are not flattering portraits of Puritanism. Certainly these books have contributed largely to the spectral aspect which Puritanism wears today in the popular mind. And even the more reflective literary critics have not taken Hawthorne's moralizing upon these portraits very seriously or literally. The portraits have made their impression independently of the author's comments upon them, and even when the comments are considered they are usually regarded as doctrines imposed upon the themes externally by a nineteenth-century mind, not as morals inherent in the subject-matter itself. There is abundant evidence, on the contrary, that Hawthorne was genuinely immersed in his subject and that he spoke of Puritanism in Puritan terms.

One of his earliest tales on Puritan themes was the *Maypole of Merry Mount*, in which he describes the suppression of an innocent May-day celebration.[17] The story closes with this significant paragraph:

"And Endicott, the severest Puritan of all who laid the rock foundation of New England, lifted the wreath of roses from the ruin of the Maypole, and threw it, with his own gauntleted hand, over the heads of the

[17] See the account of this incident given above, pp. 81-2.

Lord and Lady of the May. It was a deed of prophecy. As the moral gloom of the world overpowers all systematic gayety, even so was their home of wild mirth made desolate amid the sad forest. They returned to it no more. But as their flowery garland was wreathed of the brightest roses that had grown there, so, in the tie that united them, were intertwined all the purest and best of their early joys. They went heavenward, supporting each other along the difficult path which it was their lot to tread, and never wasted one regretful thought on the vanities of Merry Mount."

Here Puritanism clearly represents the maturity of the human mind; it is the awakening of the mind to "moral gloom" after its childish dreams of natural bliss are dissipated. The same theme is given more elaborate treatment in *The Scarlet Letter*. Hester and Dimmesdale meet in the woods for a few moments of bliss, during which they dream of living an idyllic existence far from social responsibilities; then they return to the town and undergo the consequences of their sin. At the culmination of his public disgrace and shame Dimmesdale says: "Is not this better than what we dreamed of in the forest?"

While working on *The Marble Faun*, in which the same theme is given a somewhat more romantic treatment, Hawthorne wrote: "The entire system of man's affairs, as at present established, is built up purposely to exclude the careless and happy soul. The very children would upbraid the wretched individual who should endeavor to take life and the world as—what we might naturally suppose them meant for—a place and opportunity for enjoyment." [18] Here Hawthorne's treatment of the moral order and sin is thoroughly Puritan. For him sin is an absolute and conspicuous fact, to deny which is foolish. Its consequences are inevitable and to seek escape from them is childish. The only relief from sin comes from public confession. Anything private or concealed works internally until it destroys the sinner's soul. Hawthorne puts it boldly: "Be true! Be true! Be true! Show freely to the world, if not your worst, yet some trait whereby the worst may be inferred!" [19]

The irony in these passages almost compels the modern reader to interpret them as veiled satires and to regard Hawthorne as one more transcendental reformer in spite of himself. The phrase, cited above, "system of man's affairs, *as at present established,*" seems to support such an interpretation. But the evidence on the whole is strongly to the contrary. His amusement over the Brook Farm venture, his attitude toward slavery and the Civil War, and his *laissez faire* theories in general, reveal him as a hardened realist. He did not believe in doing good, nor in "a complicated scheme of progress, which can only result in our arrival at a colder and drearier region than we were born in. It insists upon everybody's adding somewhat—a mite, perhaps, but earned by incessant effort, to an accumulated pile of usefulness, of which the only use will be

[18] Quoted in Morris: *The Rebellious Puritan*, p. 331.
[19] *The Scarlet Letter*, Chapter XXIV.

to burden our posterity with even heavier thoughts and
more inordinate labor than our own. . . . We go all
wrong by too strenuous a resolution to go all right."[20]
From the popular doctrine of reform, he returned to
the Puritan doctrine of divine sovereignty. "Vengeance
and beneficence are things that God claims for Himself. His instruments have no consciousness of His purpose; if they imagine they have, it is a pretty sure
token that they are *not* His instruments. The good of
others, like our own happiness, is not to be attained by
direct effort, but incidentally. All history and observation confirm this. I am really too humble to think of
doing good! . . . God's ways are in nothing more mysterious than in this matter of trying to do good."[21]

If further evidence of his revolt against the Mather-
Franklin philosophy of doing good is desired, it can
be found throughout his stories. The most hideous sin
is that of prying into the lives of others, of "violating
the sanctity of a soul." Chillingworth is his classic
example. Let each man search his own soul and bare
it to God and to his fellows. This is the substance of
Hawthorne's philosophy, as it was of Calvinism before it became corrupted by ecclesiastical politicians like
Cotton Mather. It is the gospel as preached by Edwards, the concern of each soul for its own salvation
and the sense of one's own worthlessness in the sight
of God. It is not the gospel of benevolence and progress, of doing good to others. Like Edwards, Haw-

[20] Quoted in Morris: *The Rebellious Puritan*, pp. 331-2.
[21] *Ibid.*, p. 310.

thorne carried the idea to its logical conclusion. The punishment of sin is not man's concern; God, or nature, sees to it. Man's business is to admit his sinfulness and to glorify God in his punishment. In *The Scarlet Letter,* Dimmesdale says to Hester: "The law we broke!—the sin here so awfully revealed!—let these alone be in thy thoughts! I fear! I fear! It may be that, when we forgot our God,—when we violated our reverence each for the other's soul,—it was thenceforth vain to hope that we could meet hereafter, in an everlasting and pure union. God knows; and He is merciful! He hath proved his mercy, most of all, in my afflictions. By giving me this burning torture to bear upon my breast! By sending yonder dark and terrible old man, to keep the torture always at red-heat! By bringing me hither to die this death of triumphant ignominy before the people! Had either of these agonies been wanting, I had been lost forever! Praised be his name! His will be done!" [22] And at the Last Judgment—"at the last day, I presume, that is, in all future days, when we see ourselves as we are—man's only inexorable judge will be himself, and the punishment of his sins will be the perception of them." [23]

Needless to say, Hawthorne used the theological terminology metaphorically. He did not need to believe in Puritanism, for he understood it. He saw the empirical truth behind the Calvinist symbols. He recovered what Puritans professed but seldom practiced—the

[22] *The Scarlet Letter,* end of Chapter XXIII.
[23] Quoted in Morris: *The Rebellious Puritan,* p. 321.

spirit of piety, humility and tragedy in the face of the inscrutable ways of God.

Though he saw the truth of this philosophy exhibited in the early history of Puritanism, he did not feel its power until he lived in Rome. There he found piety still alive, which in New England had become enshrined as mere "moral gloom." With Hawthorne the last vestiges of Puritanism emigrated from Salem. Circumstance forced him later to return to America against his will, and when he returned, it was not to Salem but to Concord that he went—Concord, the center of America's new faith and optimistic philosophy. There he was buried.

After the funeral, Emerson wrote: "Clarke in the church said that Hawthorne had done more justice than any other to the shades of life, shown a sympathy with the crime in our nature, and, like Jesus, was the friend of sinners. I thought there was a tragic element in the event that might be more fully rendered,—in the painful solitude of the man, which, I suppose, could not longer be endured, and he died of it. I have found in his death a surprise and disappointment. I thought him a greater man than any of his works betray, that there was still a great deal of work in him, and that he might some day show a purer power. . . . It would have been a happiness, doubtless, to both of us, to have come into habits of unreserved intercourse. It was easy to talk with him—there were no barriers—only he said so little, that I talked too much, and stopped only because, as he gave no indications, I

feared to exceed. He showed no egotism or self-asser-
tion, rather a humility." [24]

Apparently Emerson thought Hawthorne was really
buried. But the last judgment is not yet, and these
"friends of sinners" have a way of returning to mock
the words of kind condescension spoken at their
funerals. And now that Emerson is dead or dying, the
solitary Puritan who "said so little," has an opportunity
of "showing his purer power." Whenever self-reliance
fails, as it sooner or later must, and sinners see themselves as God sees them, piety becomes reincarnate,
though the language in which it finds expression may
bear little resemblance to that of the Puritans. But
whenever sinners become convinced that they are instruments in the hand of God, elected to carry out his holy
will, they lose their piety and begin doing good to
others. This is an ancient story, and as long as there
are sinners, the story of the Puritans will be but one
illustration of a universal theme.

[24] *Journals of Ralph Waldo Emerson, with annotations,* edited by E. W.
Emerson and W. E. Forbes (Boston, 1914), Vol. X, pp. 39-40. May 24,
1864.

INDEX

Addison, *Spectator*, 238

Anglican, 13, 55, 67; Church, 165 *f.*, 188 *f.*; clergy, 182; divines, 164

Anti-Christ, The, 11, 28, 126

Antinomians, 37, 69 *f.*

Aristotelian ethics, 253

Arminian, 179

Augustine, Saint, *City of God*, 11, 106

Bacon, Lord Francis, 162

Barrowists, 95

Baxter, Richard, 13; *The Holy Commonwealth*, 14, 17, 25, 27

Bellamy, Joseph, 215, 221, 231 *f.*; *Experimental Religion*, 209; *The Half-Way Covenant*, 210; on holy love, 213; on sin, 226 *ff.*; on the Work of Christ, 228

Bentley, William, 203 *f.*

Berkeley, Bishop George, 177 *ff.*

Bible, The, 26, 52 *f.*, 159, 192

Bishops, 166

Boston, relation to liberalism, 202 *f.*

Bradford, Governor William, 22, 29

Brattle Street Church, 88 *f.*

Brattle, Thomas, 87

Brattle, William, 87

Brook Farm, 260

Brownists, 95

Calvin, John, 18

Cambridge Platform, The, 19 *f.*, 23 *ff.*, 86

Catholic Church, The Roman, 11, 56

Channing, William Ellery, 233 *ff.*

Chauncy, Charles, 123, 157, 226; *Benevolence of the Deity*, 198 *ff.*; *Salvation of All Men*, 200, 231

Church, The, admission into, 20 *f.*; and state, 23 *ff.*; attendance, 75;

membership in, 74 *ff.*, 86, 211, 219; ordination, 29

Church of England, 157. See also *Anglican*

Clap, Captain Roger, 33

Clark, Peter, 225

Clarke, 194, 198

Collins, 178

Colman, Benjamin, 88, 94

Cotton, John, 18, 39 *f.*; against Williams, 58 *f.*, 66, 74; and Anne Hutchinson, 60, 66

Covenants, The three, 19 *ff.*, 61 *ff.*, 86

Defoe, *Essays*, 238

Deism, 157, 164. 178, 192, 195n, 197, 227, 240 *f.*

Democracy, 96 *f.*

Devil, The, and child-birth, 50; and the Indians, 37, 40; and pestilence, 38

Dickinson, Jonathan, 171

Dummer Library, 162, 164, 193

Dwight, Timothy, 207, 221, 233 *f.*

Edwards, Jonathan, 102, 164, 210, 222, 232 *f.*, 254n, 256; and theocracy, 106 *f.*, 127; his religion, 106; youthful meditations, 106; conversion to Calvinism, 108 *f.*; religious growth, 109, 112, 116; at Yale, 113, 135; and Sarah Pierrepont, 115; and the Great Awakening, 118, 123, 126; *Treatise on the Religious Affections*, 123; and Communion, 128 *ff.*; scientific and philosophical work, 135 *ff.*; philosophy and theology, 142; *The Nature of True Virtue*, 143; his Calvinism, 147 *f.*; on the will, 149 *f.*, 176, 179, 223; on final things, 151 *f.*;

265

INDEX

INDEX

Mather, Increase, 43, 87 *ff.*, 92, 94 *f.*
Mather, Samuel, 29, 96
Mayhew, Experience, 192
Mayhew, Jonathan, 170, 194, 198, 213, 218; deism and liberalism, 157 *f.*, 192, 197; Arminianism, 194 *f.*; and politics, 194, 196; *Striving*, 196; and bishops, 196
Ministerial conventions, 65, 86
Morton, Thomas, 80 *ff.*

National Church, Plan for, 95
New England Courant, The, 237
"New Lights," 156, 194
"New Theology," The, 217
Newton, Sir Isaac, 135 *ff.*, 158, 178

Original Sin, 223 *ff.*

Persecution, 51 *f.*, 64, 67
Philosophy, of history, 9, 27 *ff.*, 52, 97; of nature, 42 *ff.*, of the new period, 157 *f.*; of religion, 47 *f.*, 135
Plato, 20, 36
Polities, rival, 18, 95
Pufendorf, *De Iure*, 96
Puritan, appeal to Biblical authority, 26, 52; clergy, 9, 14 *f.*, 157; exodus, 8 *f.*; future, 264; ideal, 17; law, 27; learning, 158 *ff.*; medievalism, 11 *ff.*; morals, 254; theocracy and democracy, 29 *f.*, 97; view of Providence, 33 *f.*, 262 *f.*
Puritans, and other sects, 56, 67 *ff.*

Quakers, 60, 67, 69, 73

Rationalism, 152, 192, 228
Regeneration, 175, 215, 220 *f.*, 230
Religion, decline of, 82 *ff.*, 98, 101, 221, 240 *f.*; revolution in, 202 *f.*, 206
Revolution, The American, 157, 197, 201, 231

Saints, kinds of, 218 *f.*
Salèm, commerce of, 203
Saybrook Platform, 95
Separatists, 95, 156
Shepard, Thomas, *Autobiography*, 40 *f.*, 78 *f.*
Shorter Catechism, The, 99 *f.*
Sin and salvation, 196, 215 *ff.*, 226 *ff.*
Social life, evolution of, 80 *ff.*, 90
Society of Free and Easy, The, 250
Stiles, Ezra, 209
Stoddard, Solomon, 91 *f.*, 94 *f.*, 102, 117, 132
Stoughton, William, 86n
Synods, 65 *ff.*, 86, 95

Taylor, Nathaniel W., 236
Theocracy, 29 *f.*; and autocracy, 67, 77; decline of, 80, 106 *f.*; troubles of, 51, 64. See also *Holy Commonwealth.*
Theology, 106, 208, 222, 240 *f.*
Tories and Whigs, 157, 188, 191, 194, 257
Transcendentalists, 257

Unitarians, 235
Universalism, 200, 206 *f.*, 232

Ward, Nathaniel, 67 *f.*
Webster, Samuel, 224
Whitaker, Nathanael, 220
Whitefield, George, 122, 167, 194, 247, 255
Willard, Samuel, 98 *ff.*
Williams, Roger, 54 *f.*, 70; against John Cotton, 58 *f.*
Winthrop, Governor John, 55
Wise, John, 94 *ff.*; and democracy, 97; on natural law and civil liberty, 96
Witches, 41 *f.*, 49
Works, unregenerate, 214

Yale College, 209 *f.*

ANN ARBOR PAPERBACKS

reissues of works of enduring merit

The University of Michigan Press / Ann Arbor